INVOLUNTARY STRANGERS

On earth I am a stranger grown,
I wander in the ways of men,
Alike unknowing and unknown.

R. Burns.

INVOLUNTARY STRANGERS

Autism: The problems faced by parents

by Peggie Everard

John Clare Books
London

First published in Great Britain by John Clare Books,
106 Cheyne Walk, London, SW10 0JR

© Peggie Everard 1980

ISBN 906549 10 8

Printed & bound in Great Britain by
A. Wheaton & Co. Ltd., Exeter

Contents

Foreword

Every family is unique and the manner in which it can accept adversity or worry is different. Every parent is an individual. Sometimes both parents are equally concerned and able to care for their handicapped child; sometimes it is the mother who is best fitted to stand the strain, sometimes the father. Sometimes neither can cope. Moreover the kind of handicap makes a difference and some parents who could face the problems a physically handicapped child poses may find that they are not able to face the stigma and strain of caring for one who is mentally handicapped.

But such a child may not be the tragedy some people imagine. Most parents, I think, would acknowledge that the early years of the child's life were unhappy ones and almost all of us worry about the future, for the time when we are no longer able to protect or guide our child because of our infirmity and death. But there are many years when we carry on from day to day without too much stress, living what appears a normal life since it is the only life we know.

The reader is asked to bear with some repetition. In the first part of the book the description of the handicap, problems of diagnosis, of education and behaviour are taken from personal experience. In the second, an effort has been made to give a more technical description of these same aspects and one which covers all degrees of handicap. It is inevitable that part of the ground has been covered twice albeit from different aspects, as David is—and our experiences have been—in many ways typical. I have attempted to show what it is like living with such a child before going on to describe and discuss the problems in a wider context, to give information on the work of the National Society for Autistic Children and how it can help parents of autistic children and adults and those who are professionally involved with them.

Part I

Introduction

Each child, handicapped or normal, is an individual with his own unique personality and every handicapped child has his own degree of handicap. This is the story of an autistic child; one of the few autistic children with normal nonverbal intelligence.

Autistic children vary considerably in their abilities. Some show no skill in any field. Some may have a single skill, perhaps at drawing or numbers. A few are more socially aware but lack academic ability. However they all have one thing in common—lack of ability to communicate normally with others. Many have a quality of strangeness from the moment of birth and most have suffered from severe behaviour disturbances which were particularly bizarre before the age of five years.

There are autistic children less handicapped than David and very many who are more severely affected so that no other autistic child will show quite the same pattern of behaviour, academic ability and speech but to those parents who have an autistic child or to those who teach them, many of the incidents recorded here will be familiar.

CHAPTER ONE

Our Other Son

Before I write of our autistic child David, I should like to talk a little of our younger son Paul, who was not without problems though they were of a less serious nature. It has not yet been established, but it is possible that there is a connection between autism and Paul's handicap dyslexia. However, dyslexia or specific reading delay, is quite a common condition so that it is not surprising that many autistic children have brothers or sisters who show the characteristic reading or spelling difficulties (see Part II Chapter 17). Further research will be needed before a connection, if any, between the two conditions can be established.

Paul arrived when David was 19 months old. He was an exceptionally easy baby to care for, almost too easy I have since been told. He lay in his pram or cot until I was ready to feed him, always seemed content and was quite happy to be left on his own. However, he laughed and gurgled and was very responsive. He had a mischievous smile and an elfin prettiness.

Paul was instantly attractive to other people. I didn't realise it at the time but this was not only because of his looks but because of his responsiveness and his awareness of others. Before he was a year old he seemed to know everything that was happening. On the whole his motor development was a little behind David's at the same age. He was smaller and not so strongly built and his head needed more support. He was later cutting his teeth and could not sit until he was eight months old and even then had a tendency to overbalance. He never developed any great skill at crawling but hitched himself along; first on his bottom and then on two hands and one knee. However, he learned to

walk at 17 months, 2 months earlier than David, had good
balance and was very much more nimble.

When Paul was about 18 months old I realised that people
were beginning to worry because he, like his brother, wasn't
speaking. But Paul was very different from David so that in
spite of his lack of speech, I couldn't bring myself to feel any
deep concern. Perhaps worrying over one child is enough for
anyone. If Paul had been an only child it might have been
another matter. Seeing the two of them together it seemed to
me that there could not be anything very wrong with him; he
somehow picked clues out of the air and made himself
understood. He was a paid up member of the family, while
David was on the periphery, never quite belonging.

When Paul was two years and 10 months old, he said his
first word—'lorry'. He had a passion for cars, lorries and
dustcarts—in fact anything that had an engine and ran on
wheels. He didn't speak again until he was three so that he
and David really started to talk at about the same time.
Some of his words were clear, but others were quite wrongly
pronounced. He used sentences almost immediately and his
intonation was normal. He chattered away happily to
anyone who would listen. My husband could understand
him some of the time, I could most of the time and other
people couldn't understand him at all—or not at first. At his
nursery school they were pleased with his progress but were
worried about the jargon.

I remember the holiday we spent before his fourth
birthday. We stopped to speak to a friend and he told her,
much to her mystification, that we'd been round a 'torten
and under a lorter line'. We had no problem in translating
this into 'round a corner and under a railway line', as he
always used the same sounds to represent the same object.
However, I found it strange that he couldn't tell the
difference. If I asked him to say 'railway' he said 'lorter' and
was perfectly satisfied with this.

By the time he was four everyone could understand what
he was saying and I imagined our troubles were over as far as
he was concerned.

As Paul grew towards school age I thought I would teach him his letters. I had enjoyed teaching David and looked forward to a similar experience with Paul. He was such a bright, quick child and, I thought, would learn so easily. But I was wrong. I showed the letters to him over and over again, but he couldn't remember them. I realised that I would lose my temper if I persisted, so I stopped trying to teach him. I decided it was something better left to the primary school.

He started school at 5¼, very late by present day standards and late even at the end of the 1950's. It was a large primary school further away than the nursery he had been attending. Although the school was in a bright, modern building it didn't have a bright modern outlook. There was a notice by the main door saying 'Parents must not proceed beyond this point'. One mother, worried about her child, wanted to speak to the headmistress in December and was told that she must wait until the school Open Day in June. The children were 'streamed' during their first year which seemed a little unnecessary. For children who were bright and had no learning problems it was a good school with an excellent record for gaining grammar school places and for slow learners without handicap it was also suitable as they were taught at their own pace, but there was no time for children who didn't fit the system, the school was too large to take account of misfits, for bright or slow children with specific disabilities. Paul hated it. He hadn't been there long before he was kept in for some misdemeanour or other practically every day. As one couldn't speak to the teachers or head except for one day in the year it was difficult to find out what the trouble was, though as time wore on it became apparent that the teacher was finding Paul difficult to teach—just as I had.

Between five and seven years old the children were taught the 'look and say' method of reading and I don't think Paul ever made head or tail of this. He learned the shapes of letters and could write his name neatly and clearly, but strangely, if given a clean sheet of paper he was likely to write from right to left, so that one had to hold the paper up to a glass to read what he had written. Even more strangely he couldn't tell when he was doing this. He has to ask me whether he was writing the right way round. I was told that this was not uncommon in left-handed children. It is, so I was told, more natural to move the pencil away from the body—that is, from left to right in a right handed person (and the reverse, of course for those who are left handed). I can't quite see why this should be as far as I know Arabs and Indians have no marked directional difficulties, however I found that if I made a mark on the left hand margin of the page so that he had some indication where to start writing, then he wrote correctly, from left to right.

The Harley Street doctor whom I had taken David to and who had started us off on our long search for a diagnosis, had kept in touch although we could not afford to visit him again. Though he had been instrumental in helping us to get David diagnosed he was the first to admit that he didn't understand the problem, but he was most interested in Paul. He told me that in his opinion he was dyslexic and gave me a list of books on this subject to read. Paul fitted the picture only too well. It accounted for his slowness in talking and his jargon.

Paul, not unnaturally, began to hate school and would complain of tummy aches and odd pains in the morning. As he suffered from recurrent attacks of biliousness I had to make up my mind whether these were real pains or not. Sometimes I would keep him at home only to find that by eleven, when there was no danger that I would take him, he would be full of health and energy.

I learned to dread the school Open Days. Each parent went to the appropriate classroom and was given a numbered card; this was the order in which one spoke to the class teacher. After the first year I would go late and get a high number. A low one meant a whole roomful of parents listening to the teacher while ostensibly looking at the work on display. It was meant to be a private interview but within the confines of a small classroom most of what was said could be heard. No doubt if only praise were to be metered out I shouldn't have minded but it seemed that Paul was mischievous, had no interest in learning, was naughty, made no effort and fooled around at the back of the classroom distracting the other children. I saw the headmistress several times and explained that he had problems with reading and tried to tell her what they were but she felt that he was a bright child who had more interest in fooling around than in getting down to work, so I gave up.

Paul was extraordinarily nimble and was terrifying to watch—so, as far as possible, I didn't. He was a most active and efficient climber. Though accident prone in other directions, he never fell doing this. In the park behind our house were great tall trees and he would go up them almost to the top, testing each branch carefully. He would come and ask me to go out and watch him and I would dutifully go and try not to look. He would come downstairs by swinging over the landing banisters and would then hang and drop to the floor. I became so used to this that it seemed normal. It wasn't until a friend saw him do it and was terrified that I realised it was, perhaps, a little unusual.

At seven, Paul was taught phonetics and began to see what reading was all about. However, his progress was still slow. He was writing the occasional letter backwards but not very often. His script was neat enough but he started each letter from the wrong end which meant that he was unable to do 'joined up' writing. His delay in reading was particularly vexing as, unlike David, he had no gift for science or numbers but liked stories and words and had an intuitive understanding of the feelings and emotions of others. He was still unhappy at school and his progress was painfully slow. Although he was reading after a fashion I still had complaints about his behaviour. At home I didn't find him difficult although one always had to be one jump ahead of him. A year or so before we'd had interminable arguments as to whether he would or would not wear his mac but he'd learnt to avoid confrontations and it took me a little while to realise he always managed to get his own way. However, he was a companionable child and didn't present any serious

behaviour problems. He had two annoying habits which he
knew I could not do anything about. He would refuse to
come home when we were out which meant I had either to
drag him away screaming or give in which went against the
grain. Or he would sometimes behave badly when we went
out to tea knowing that I would find it difficult to reprimand
him. Both these irritating traits were overcome when I was
able to walk away and leave him to find his own way home—
or leave him at home without supervision. But he wasn't
really any more difficult than most of my friends' children.
His behaviour problems were mainly centred around school.
We decided to take him away from the large primary school
where he had spent 3½ unhappy years.

For a year Paul went to the convent which David attended
and where, for the first time, he went willingly to school. And
then when David left Paul left as well. I had visited our local
Church of England primary school and had decided to send
him there. He was old enough now to cross the busy road after
he'd left the bus; there was a central refuge which made this
fairly easy. He then had quite a long walk but never
complained, as I expected him to. It was a small school, very
modern, as the older children had only recently moved from
the Victorian building just down the road. In fact, the young
children were still there. There were only four classes and
four teachers, one woman and three men which was unusual
in a primary school. In the very large school he had first
attended, there were no men. Even the head had been a
woman.

For the first time in his life Paul really liked school. The
teaching was formal and though the children were well
disciplined, the teachers were kind. I don't think they really
understood Paul's problems, but, as at the convent, they saw
him as an individual and were always considerate. Again, I
was told, at first, that he was mischievous but I never felt
they blamed me for this but rather that if they had a problem
teaching him then it was they who must try to find out why.
(I realised how difficult he must be when one of the masters
remarked that he had been sitting just behind Paul on the

bus one day and was surprised to see how well he behaved. I
was astounded. Why would Paul behave badly on a bus?)
For children who have learning problems the small school
seems to be the answer. There may be exceptions, I'm sure
there are, and a lot must depend on the way a school is run.
However, in a large school, even if the class is small, the child
does not become known as an individual in quite the same
way.

It was at this time that I read that the Invalid Children's
Aid Association was taking an interest in children with
dyslexia and was attempting to find out the extent of the
handicap and how it differed from other reading problems or
indeed *if* it did. I wrote to them and asked if I could take Paul
to see the specialist who was studying this for them. In a
short time an appointment was arranged.

I can't remember all the tests Paul was given. He had an
IQ test and it was found that his intelligence was
comfortably above average on both language and
performance. Although not within the genius range it was
well within that needed for placement at a grammar school.

The doctor asked Paul to indicate his own left hand,
which, after a moment's thought, he did. Then the doctor,
who was standing in front of and facing Paul, asked him to
point out his (the doctor's) left hand. Paul pointed to his
right.

Paul is very firmly left handed. The only thing he does
with his right hand, which a right handed person would do is
to eat with his knife and fork in his right and left hand
respectively. If he uses a knife, fork or spoon on its own, then
he uses it in his left hand. Everything is reversed. He cannot
use a clip on and turn type of tin opener or a potato peeler
intended for a right handed person. Paul is not only left
handed, he is left footed, which was quite obvious when he
was asked to kick a ball. His right eye was shown to be
dominant however. It is thought that it may be this cross
laterality that is responsible for children having this type of
reading problem.

I told the doctor of his delay in talking, the jargon, his

difficulties with reading and the way I had had to mark the left hand side of the page before he knew which side to start writing. The doctor was interested in this and murmured that this would indicate a directional difficulty. At this time Paul hadn't quite caught up in his reading but his main problem was spelling. He had begun to write in a small script very difficult to read, which I felt he used to hide his spelling mistakes. I was asked if he liked team games. He didn't and would do his best to get out of them. However, he was reasonably athletic and in sports which did not involve catching, hitting or kicking a ball but were self initiated such as running, climbing or swimming he was very good. He had recently grown out of twisting words. When he was younger he would say 'breakfats' for 'breakfast', 'dicifult' for 'difficult', 'takeover' for 'overtake', 'Christmas' for 'Easter', 'blue' for 'yellow' and would make many other reversals and errors. When he read he appeared not to be able to scan a word from left to right; muddling the letters in short words— such as reading 'sawn' for 'swan' and guessing at words of several syllables. All this, it seemed, was very typical of the problem known as dyslexia. I agreed to take him up to London for spelling lessons once a week.

He had an hour's lesson at a London hospital and was given a list of irregular words to learn which he would be expected to know by the following week. He didn't have a lot of homework so I would make sure that we spent fifteen minutes every evening on his spelling. He loved stories and because of his difficulties, I read to him every night for years in an effort to keep him abreast of his contemporaries. I wanted him to like books. I think I enjoyed these reading sessions as much as he did and I became particularly fond of the Jennings books. It was quite a disappointment when he took over and started reading on his own. However, when he did this I realised that the worst of his problems were over.

The spelling lessons came to an end when Paul left the small Church school. The eleven plus was still in force and it was obvious that Paul would not get a grammar school place. As we knew we couldn't expect this, we never told him about it, though he must have realised that there was something afoot. The children were given a number of tests and examinations so that they did not know which of these were the real thing.

We had been making enquiries about the secondary schools in our borough. The one recommended by the headmaster was a school which was three miles from us in a rather rough area. It had an excellent reputation, however. The children were well disciplined and although it was some distance away and had over 900 pupils (a lot before the days of large comprehensives, though all the secondary schools seemed large after the little Church school) it seemed the best choice. Although able to stand up for himself at a small school, the headmaster felt he would not be able to cope with gang warfare and it seemed that this would be less likely at the school he helped us choose.

Paul was improving; he had benefited from his spelling lessons. He could at least make a stab at finding the words he wanted in the dictionary and his spelling was not bizarre, merely bad, though improving. His rote memory was poor and he was very weak at figures.

I explained Paul's difficulty with reading and spelling but I am not sure how effective this was, though he was allowed to use a tables chart in maths lessons. As the school was large it seemed it was not easy for them to make allowances for anyone except for those who showed more obvious physical disabilities. Paul's happiest days at school were over. He stayed until he was almost 18 but he was glad to leave. Basically his best subject was English and as soon as he began to read fluently he made big strides. When given a book intended to last the term, and adult one, such as H.E. Bates' 'Fair Stood the Wind for France' he would bring it home and read it in two or three evenings. In spite of poor spelling he enjoyed creative writing and was good at it, showing insight into people's motives and emotions and a vivid imagination.

Very much to our surprise Paul got 3 good O levels and 6 CSE's all but one at grade 2. This may not seem an

overwhelming achievement to parents who have children
who get 9 O levels with ease and top that up with 2 or 3 A's
but we never expected him to get anything.

Paul stayed on at school virtually doing nothing during
the last year and then quietly found himself a job, after
studying careers books, in the civil service in Whitehall. He
made up his own mind, made his own application and took
himself for the interview. He didn't want us to help him in
any way. Between 16–17 we had had a few battles, which we
had lost, over the length of his hair and a few arguments as to
what time he should get in at night. The usual battles in fact.
He also decided, at 17, that he was old enough to choose his
own clothes (apart from school uniform). Everything at this
time had to be black; trousers and jacket as well as pullovers,
though he did choose a bright orange shirt.

On the whole though, we had few problems with him as he
grew older. Whether having a handicapped brother made
him more mature than most young people it is impossible to
say but we were fortunate that he did not seem to feel the
need to rebel as so many of his contemporaries did.

CHAPTER TWO

David

David is now 28 years old. He was born in March after a normal pregnancy, though a rather long labour, weighing over 8lbs. At birth he did not have the red crumpled look of the newly born and a little prompting was needed to get him to cry. Even more prompting was needed to get him to stay awake long enough to feed. But when he was awake it was difficult, indeed impossible, to stop him from crying. He stopped when he was ready and not before; nothing that I did had any effect. David was our first child and I had no experience of babies so I assumed that this was due entirely to my own mishandling. I had unbounded admiration for mothers whose babies stopped crying immediately when rocked or picked up. Between birth and six weeks old he had two short episodes of cyanosis.

However, after the first 3 months David became much easier to handle. He fed well and settled into a routine. From a rather pale and sickly infant he emerged plump and pink, the very epitome of babyhood. He laughed when tickled, liked being picked up and apparently loved everyone—and yet there must have been something to make me uneasy for when he was about eight months old I remember telling the doctor at the clinic that I was anxious. His motor milestones were normal and I had no problems getting him on to solid food. I recollect that I was made to feel a little odd for querying his progress. By the time he was between 10–12 months old I began to worry more actively and yet could not pinpoint why I was worried. I was sure something was wrong but whatever it was eluded me. But I remembered that even at the hospital where he was born he had been different from the other babies; disinclined to feed or to sleep at the expected times. One nurse had accused me of not trying to feed him. From the first I had felt inept. When I returned to the hospital for the usual six week post-natal check up David screamed all the time we were there and refused to be pacified. I noticed that other mothers did not seem to have any problems. Their babies stopped crying when they were comforted.

When he was a year old he became terrified of unshaded electric light bulbs whether the light was switched on or off. When taken into a room the first thing he did was to look to see whether there was a shade and if there wasn't he would scream. Fortunately lights are normally shaded but we went once to see friends who had moved house and were still in the process of settling in. The visit was a disaster.

From the age of 12 months on he became progressively more strange. He began to scream when he woke from his midday sleep. I became adept at having his meal ready to shovel into his mouth as soon as he woke. Very occasionally this succeeded, but more often it didn't and once he started he would scream for an hour or more without stopping. He could be heard for quite a distance in our quiet surburban road and I was aware of the comments of neighbours. At this time, too, he began to rock in his pram or cot. He would wake at about 5.30 a.m. and begin bouncing. My husband and I both sleep very soundly so we didn't hear him but unfortunately our neighbours did and loud knocks on the dividing wall would get us out of bed in an attempt to anchor the cot so that he could not move it. We never succeeded. This led to deteriorating relations with our neighbours and to David sleeping in every room except the kitchen in an effort to keep him from disturbing their sleep.

Bouncing in the pram was less of a nuisance to others. Fortunately it was a sturdy well built one with no tendency to overbalance and he would bounce it along until it would go no further because of a wall or other obstruction and continue to bounce. The back of the pram became very battered of course though it withstood a remarkable amount of punishment. It was about this time too that my neighbour asked me if I thought David suffered from earache as he would sit and hold one ear and scratch the pram cover with his other hand. It became obvious later that he enjoyed listening to sounds.

At 12 months old David did not put things into his mouth as most babies do. He made no attempt to feed himself and later, when he did begin to eat rusks or biscuits, he would nibble round and round them until he was left with a small damp piece in the middle of his hand which he had no idea how to dispose of. He learned to drink from a cup quite normally but at about eight months he choked and refused to use a cup again. From then on he drank from a tablespoon and continued with this even after I stopped giving him a bedtime bottle at 12 months. I don't know how long this would have gone on if we hadn't had a very warm night when he was about 15 months old. A friend of mine was with me when David started crying. By this time I suffered a severe lack of confidence at being able to fathom any reason for his screams and even if, by some stroke of luck, I should find a cause, I doubted my ability to stop him. My friend, unaware of any problem, suggested he was thirsty and gave him a glass of water which he drank down in one gulp. After that I had no further trouble.

It was at about this age that David almost imperceptibly began to drift away. He began to look 'through' rather than 'at' us. I could sense it happening but seemed powerless to stop it. He appeared to be aware of it too as he would want me to hold his hand when I was wheeling his pram along. By the time he was three or three and a half years old he couldn't recognise me or my husband and seemed quite unaware of everything that was going on around him.

When David was 19 months old his brother Paul arrived. Paul was born at home so there was no separation. David appeared uninterested or unaware of the new baby and although he crawled across the bed and had a quick look in the carry-cot he showed no other reaction and took no further notice of him.

David crawled with amazing speed. It was partly this that convinced our GP that there couldn't be anything wrong with him. He was a heavy child and didn't walk until he was 19 months old, about a week after Paul was born. He was very unsteady and walked with his feet widely spaced for quite a while but gradually became more proficient at balancing. For some time, although it didn't happen very often, he would lean forward as he walked as if he were going to fall on his face. This would last for a few steps and then he would regain his balance.

David was handsome rather than pretty. His appearance has changed remarkably little and he is still, unlike Paul, recognisable from his childhood photographs. He hadn't Paul's responsiveness and appeared stolid, taking very little notice of other people. It is easy to see, now that I understand David's problem, that this lack of awareness was the very thing I was unable to pinpoint and which had made me uneasy.

I was fortunate that Paul was such a contented baby because David was becoming more and more of a problem. His behaviour was bizarre; he was somehow unreachable. He was difficult to take out because he would touch everything. He would grab things from shelves, tip things over, run behind counters in shops and into people's gardens or houses if the front doors were left open and because he ignored me when I tried to stop him, he appeared thoroughly spoilt. However, he was very advanced in his play with educational toys. At 15 months he could sort out nesting jars with amazing speed and dexterity and by two years old he was playing with toys intended for school age children. Although his gross movements were clumsy and his balance was poor so that he was afraid of falling over and hurting himself, his fine movements were deft.

Just before he was two years old we visited friends who had a child a little younger and it was when I was watching this child I became certain that there was something seriously wrong. I knew it, but still couldn't define why. I realise now that it was the interaction with his parents—and with us too—that this child showed and which David just did not have.

The first two years are ones of utter bewilderment for parents. I think it must be worse if the autistic child is the first born as one has no experience—but this may be personal bias. One may put all oddities down to one's own inefficiency, this leads in turn to lack of confidence in handling the child and it has always seemed to me that confidence is a quality that is badly needed when dealing with a handicapped infant. I think these years must always be unhappy ones. It is so much easier to grapple with a problem if one knows what it is, but to feel that there is something wrong yet not to be able to define it, to seek help yet not to be able to explain why help is needed, to be told that everything is all right when deep down one feels that it isn't and the feeling that if anything is wrong then it must be in the way you are handling the child, is a lot for a young mother to cope with especially in the early years of marriage when one is plunged into a completely new life anyway. A named handicap, however serious, seems more bearable than not knowing.

Visits to the clinic were a strain, too. David did not seem to be like the other babies. For the first 3 months he did not gain weight as he should have done. He was very difficult to feed. At first he was half breast and half bottle fed, but it all took so long that we were up half the night, only to be up early the next morning to start again. We were exhausted. At six weeks it was suggested that he should be entirely bottle fed and this eased the situation a little—but staff at the clinic, as at the hospital, assumed the feeding problems and his lack of progress were of my making and I thought that perhaps they were right. I hated going to the clinic. I felt my inefficiencies were on public display.

At two years old the main symptom that one could point to, apart from his strangeness which was difficult to explain, was his lack of speech. He had said 'ma-ma' and 'da-da' but this had not meant anything and at 24 months he did not attempt to speak and was without babble. I went to the clinic determined to get the doctor to listen but before I had had time to speak to her, she approached me and said that in her opinion David was severely mentally retarded and that there was nothing to be done. While we were waiting to see her a dog had come into the room and had run barking, through it. David had seemed quite unaware of this incident although the dog had run right past him. I think that she may have had doubts for some time and this just clinched it.

In one way it was a relief to have some acknowledgement that there was something wrong but I was not entirely happy with the diagnosis. I didn't know much about the normal development of children or about mental deficiency but it seemed to me that David just did not fit. In some way he was different. I remembered his normal motor development, his quickness at seeing the way the catches on boxes worked and his skill with educational toys. I couldn't think what it was that was wrong, but whatever it was, it was, I felt, a condition not usually met with nor easily recognised.

When David was just over 2½ we took him to the Hospital for Sick Children in Great Ormond Street taking Paul with us. He was seen by a paediatrician—and by 30 students. The paediatrician pointed out to the students that he was unlike the retarded child that they had seen immediately before him. He asked them to note how he had taken an immediate interest in the large lead weighted doll which he'd found fascinating because it wouldn't overturn. He pointed out the way that Paul was aware of his surroundings and indeed was playing to the gallery as he usually did, and how David had not appeared to notice that there was anyone else in the room. He suspected that David was deaf. We said that we didn't think he could be as he could hear the slightest rustle of a sweet paper but the paediatrician told us that deafness took different forms and that because he could hear a sweet paper did not mean that he could hear, properly, what we were saying. We left the hospital feeling happier than we had for some time. Deafness, we felt, was something David and his family, friends and relations would learn to cope with.

A few weeks later I had a card asking me to take him for a hearing test. A friend looked after Paul and I took David up to London. The test was not a success. David did not cooperate and I was told that it was inconclusive and that I should return in six months time. The six months passed; we never heard from the hearing unit and we were back where we started. I was sure by now that he was not suffering from deafness in any form.

When David was three years old and we were getting nowhere I made an appointment to see a Harley Street specialist. He was very kind and encouraged me to give him every detail of David's development and of my worries. I talked and talked. No-one had really listened before or seemed interested in my opinions. He thought that David might be suffering from thyroid deficiency and sent us to see a specialist in this field. This specialist, one of the leading ones in the country, decided that David was not suffering from a thyroid deficiency though he did prescribe a course of tablets which David took for several months. He did, however, suggest that we might take him to see a well-known consultant paediatrician at a large London post graduate teaching hospital. This we did—and this is where we were at last given a diagnosis which sounded more convincing. The diagnosis was 'severe emotional disturbance' 'juvenile schizophrenia' and 'psychosis'. All three terms were used on different occasions, the word 'autism' was not at that time readily used or perhaps not by the consultant we saw, though we found later that this was what was meant. David was 3 years and 5 months old.

CHAPTER THREE

Very Alone

There is a great deal to be said for the closeness and warmth of the extended family. Nowadays young parents lead isolated lives and can become very lonely. This is bad enough when everything is quite normal but when support is needed and there is none available, one is very alone. Living in a new area, friends may really be acquaintances—one—knows—quite—well, rather than people with whom one has a lot in common and has known through the ups and downs of life over many years. The support of just one person is enough; someone one can talk to, a shoulder to cry on, someone who won't criticise but just *be* there. Very often I felt that other parents I talked to of my problems were not very sympathetic—almost secretly glad that it was my problem. After all, they had escaped—it might have happened to them. It was understandable enough if not very helpful. And looking back now the most outstanding memory is one of unhappiness and of being alone with my worries. My husband and I both come from small families. I was born abroad, had spent my schooldays in England separated from my parents and sister, spending holidays with relatives in different parts of the country, mostly in the south. I had few cousins of my own age (only two in effect. A third lives in South Africa and it is only recently that we've met). My parents did not live near us, at the time of our marriage they were living on the south coast. I had come to work in London and had met my husband there. He had been born and brought up in an outer London suburb and had, all his life, lived with his mother, father and brother in the house in which he'd been born. My husband had a number of aunts and uncles, mostly unmarried, living in Northamptonshire and Cornwall and had only one cousin, so between us we had few relations of our own age. Neither his brother nor my sister were married at the time, nor have they married since.

We began our new lives in a pleasant semi-detached house just round the corner from my husband's old home. It was in a secluded road, and had a large garden backing on to a quiet park. If one had to live near London, and we did, then we couldn't have lived in a pleasanter spot. The tall trees at the bottom of the garden gave an illusion of country life and the garden was full of squirrels and birdsong. My friends at that time were of necessity the wives of my husband's friends (and many became my own personal friends in due course). My own friends were widely scattered. I was very tied with two children, one of them handicapped, so it was impossible for me to see them very often. It seemed that we had to struggle through by ourselves. I found my in-laws tolerant and gentle. My mother-in-law was particularly kind to David for which I was grateful but she became very angry when I suggested that there might be something wrong. It was obvious that I would not get the support I needed there. My own family was even less help as, once it was realised that David was handicapped they did not want to have anything to do with him.

My husband ran his own small business and was usually preoccupied, furthermore he knew even less about children than I did so I had a free hand to deal with David as I saw fit.

It was when Paul was about nine months old that I had some glimmering of David's problem, though it wasn't until later that I really began to understand. It seems amazing to me now that I could have had David with me, day in day out, and not gained any real insight into the way the world appeared to him. Why do we take it for granted that all children are aware and are able to sort out what is happening around them even when their behaviour indicates that they don't? It certainly never crossed my mind that this was a possibility until David was over two years old and even then I really didn't think it through properly. On this particular occasion, Paul threw his teddy out of the

pram and I said 'Poor teddy, he's on the floor' and Paul
laughed and looked over the side of the pram at his teddy on
the carpet. It struck me at the time that David would not
have done this. He might have looked at me when I spoke, he
might have laughed but he would not have looked at his
teddy.

A month or two after this we spent a short holiday in
Dorset with friends and when we were sitting on the beach
David was asked to give me something. I think it was a safety
pin. He took it, looked at it and then dropped it in the sand.
It seemed that he did not understand the request 'Give it to
Mummy'. David was exactly 2½ years old at this time. It
was then that I made up my mind to take him to see a
specialist but before the appointment was fixed we had
another surprise holiday. My husband had to go to
Portsmouth to work for two weeks so we rented a caravan on
Hayling Island.

It was then October and the tourist season was over. The
caravan was in the back garden of a house owned by a very
pleasant couple. We had had a horrible journey down,
David was car sick nearly the whole way. He'd shown an
inclination towards this previously but never before had he
been so badly affected. We arrived feeling messy and smelly
and the only water supply was from a standpipe in the
garden.

It was at this time that David screamed every evening for
at least an hour. I could find no reason for this and had
become almost inured to it. He would stop as suddenly as he
had begun. The woman who owned the caravan could hear
him of course and she was curious. I explained his problems
and that I was taking him to see a specialist as soon as we
returned home. In this case I felt she really believed me and
was sympathetic. Sometimes one had the feeling that, quite
understandably, people thought we were mishandling or
even mistreating him.

It was while we were at Hayling Island that the tin
bending began, a habit we've never been able to eradicate
and which continues to this day. For some time he had had a

set of tin nesting jars (the previous ones had been plastic) and one day he found that he could derive enormous pleasure from manipulating the metal.

At two David had still been in touch with us to some extent. He had been capable of showing jealousy if he considered Paul was getting too much attention. But by 2½ he was becoming more withdrawn though he could still recognise me. He tapped everything he picked up and held it to his ear. He made noises in tunnels and large buildings so that he could listen to the echo. He stroked smooth surfaces and loved the feel of fur. He liked nursery rhymes in fact all music and if I felt that he might be going to scream I could just possibly stop him by singing, though I could never stop him at his routine 'screaming' time! He also had an odd habit of throwing out his right arm, after making a ball of his fist with his thumb extended and then staring at it. He was a solitary child, content to spend long hours alone. He never sought comfort if he hurt himself and he did not play with toys requiring imagination, though he was way ahead of his age with educational ones. He would also play for hours with a bowl of water, filling and emptying his tins although he wouldn't play with sand; he just ran it through his fingers. As a baby, after the first few months, he would hold out his arms to be picked up and seemed to enjoy being cuddled. He would notice when his father came home and became excited when I came in and spoke to him; he would help me to dress him by holding out the required arm or leg. But by 2½ he objected to his hand being held when we were walking. He did not like to be picked up nor would he sit on anyone's lap; he seemed afraid that he would be allowed to fall. However, he enjoyed a romp or a tickle. For a short while at this age he said 'Der-der' in an approximation of 'David' although he never tried to say anything else. He was not toilet trained and made no attempt to feed himself with a spoon, though he would use his fingers.

This year, that is from the time David was two and a half until he was three and a half, was taken up with trying to find what was wrong with him. There was really no progress to report. In fact the reverse was true, he became more and more distant. Looking back I've thought that perhaps I could have made more of an effort to stop this but Paul was taking up my time as he began to get around, first by hitching and then by walking. He was a lively child and into everything. His first smile as a baby was mischievous, and he lived up to its promise. He wasn't difficult to handle until he was two years old when he became very negative and did his best to resist conforming. He still didn't talk but we understood each other perfectly and a times there was quite a battle of wills. He was still too small to reach the door handles so that it was possible to remove him forcibly when he became too demanding. When Paul screamed we all knew why.

Although David had drifted into a world of his own where other people did not exist he was still progressing in other ways. He became very interested in the differences in musical notes, especially those which were only a semi-tone apart. He was also fascinated by letters. He would watch the credits on television and look through books, not at the pictures as one would expect, but at the print. When I went into his playroom I would find that he had sorted his lettered bricks into piles—'A's' in one place, 'D's' in another. He seemed to want to categorise things. On other occasions I would see that he had sorted his collection of sea shells into types and sizes, and objects according to colour. His main preoccupation though was in making long lines of things. He would begin with his bricks and then his other toys and lastly unattached domestic objects such as clothes brushes, kitchen spoons or anything else that he could find around the house. The line would go from the front door to the back but he didn't seem to mind when it was moved or dismantled. In spite of his apparent unawareness of all that was going on around him he knew when anything in the house was changed or moved. However he didn't object, as most autistic children do.

When he was three years and four months old David went into hospital for observation. It didn't appear to upset him, nor apparently did he miss us or recognise me when I went up to London, every other day, to visit him. He would look in my bag to see if there was anything interesting in it but that was all. It could have been upsetting and would have been if I hadn't become accustomed to him. At the end of three weeks we were told that we could take him home. The day that David had gone into hospital we had enjoyed our first outing as a normal family and had been able to go into a café for tea, something we could not have done if we'd had him with us. All the same we missed him and were glad to have him home again. As soon as he came in at the front door, he picked up where he had left off and behaved as if he had never been away.

Shortly after this, I was asked to take David to see a doctor in Harley Street who was particularly interested in children with his diagnosis. We spent more than an hour with her and David practically dismantled her room. He walked round methodically picking things up and throwing them on the floor, emptying boxes and tins, pulling books out of bookcases, pushing things off the shelves until there wasn't a spot on the floor left uncovered. I was told not to try and stop him. The doctor told me that she wasn't at all sure what was wrong with him and when I went back to see the Consultant he said that he might have been mistaken and it was possible that David was severely retarded.

At 3½ David was at his most handicapped. He had descended into a trough and it seemed impossible that he could become worse. He was completely isolated, wrapped up in his own interests. However, even when he was at his most withdrawn he would be momentarily interested in things he had never seen or heard before. I was surprised once, when we were out to see him looking up at what I thought was a plane overhead. We were near a small private airfield and he had shown no particular interest before. When I looked up, though, I saw it was a helicopter. I think this was the first he'd seen. Once having observed this phenomenon he showed no further interest. By this time though, he didn't recognise me and I could have left him in the High Street and he wouldn't have missed me nor would he have realised that he was on his own. I made up my mind then that we couldn't go on as we were; that I should have to take positive steps if there were to be any improvement in his behaviour. My days were busy but I decided to spend an hour every evening with him after Paul had gone to bed. This meant keeping him up a little later but he didn't seem to need so much sleep as other children.

It occurred to me that it was because David had stopped looking at me that he didn't recognise me. He didn't look at me when I spoke, nor did he watch my face to read my expression. Our eyes seldom met now that he was getting around on his own—so the first thing to do was to get down to his level. I spent the first evening crawling around after him handing him bricks to add to the line he was making. He was surprised and actually looked at me with interest. I felt I had made contact and wondered why I hadn't thought of doing this before. As David and I played together each evening I began to know him better and really to think hard about his handicap. It seemed to me that he didn't understand what I was saying.

A week or so after we had begun our evening sessions the children and I spent a day with a friend in a neighbouring suburb. We talked of David and his problems and she told me of the Montessori convent at the end of her road. When I left her, with the children, prepared for our three mile walk home, I decided on impulse to call in. Fortunately the Principal was there though the children and nuns had left. Paul had fallen asleep and David, as always, was content for me to leave him. She was very kind. I told her that I didn't know what was wrong with David, that he'd been diagnosed as emotionally disturbed and as severely retarded. She asked me to fetch him and I brought both children in.

David was very interested in the school equipment and the Principal asked if he was aggressive. I explained that this was the last thing he was and as if to demonstrate this, Paul took the piece of equipment that David was holding away from him. As usual David made no protest. The Principal

said that David could attend the nursery class on a trial basis
after half term at the beginning of November.

David began his school life at 3 years 7½ months old.

School

The school, which at that time took girls up to eleven and boys to seven, was not quite three miles from us. I didn't drive then and to get David there meant catching two different buses. David was only attending school from 9.20 a.m. until midday so that it seemed that we were no sooner back home, than we had to set out again to fetch him. On Fridays the Roman Catholic children went to mass and we didn't have to get to the school until 10 a.m. so I would take the big pram and walk to the school, then I would do my shopping with Paul at the local shops, drop into my friend's for a coffee, pick David up and walk home. However, I'm not sure how long I could have kept this up, it was exhausting. As it happened, it was only for two months as I had a call from the district nurse who told me that there was a vacancy in the local authority nursery for Paul. I hadn't asked for this in fact I didn't know that there was a nursery so it hadn't occurred to me. I found that a place has been found as we were considered as an 'emergency'. Nursery hours were from 9 a.m. until 3 in the afternoon. It would have suited me better if I could have fetched Paul on my way home with David at lunch time but this was not allowed. So my daily programme was to wheel them both round to the nursery school, leave the pushchair there—then take David on to school and return home. I would usually be back by 10.30 and I'd leave again at 11.15 and be home with David by 12.45 or 1 p.m. David and I would then have lunch and at 2.45 would walk round to the nursery school, pick Paul up and wheel them both home in the pushchair. This was easier, but still took up most of my day but after two months or so of this I was once more lucky. Someone else, living in our road had a son at the same school as David. He was older and stayed all day but James' father offered to take David every morning. I went with them for the first week but after that he was collected for me. This made an enormous difference. I would wait for David to go, then take Paul and be home again by 9.30. I still had to fetch David at 12 and Paul at 3 of course.

At this point neither David nor Paul were talking and David was at his very worst. When I fetched him after his first morning I was met by the nun who was to have him in her charge for the next 3 years or so. She told me that he was obviously very handicapped, but that he most certainly was not retarded in the usual way. Although the school was for normal children it was their policy to have two or three handicapped children there at any one time and the nuns were familiar with most of the more common problems. The Sister told me that David had had all the Montessori equipment out and had played with it most intelligently. This bore out what I thought and when the Sister remained enthusiastic about his unusual abilities I asked the Principal to write to the consultant. We were back to the diagnosis of emotional disturbance/juvenile schizophrenia/psychosis. The Principal and the Sister were an enormous support to me. I hadn't had any real help and encouragement before this and I gradually felt less alone with my problems. The next step was settling Paul into the nursery. Unlike David who didn't know whether I was there or not, Paul protested vigorously when left. He would cling to me and scream and his fingers would have to be disentangled from my clothes. He was only 2¼, too young to leave me really and I found it distressing, but I was assured that he was quite happy and that as soon as I left he settled down and played contentedly. They were concerned that he was not talking. Apart from that his development appeared to be quite normal. Unlike David he was almost toilet trained.

Though I was continuing my evening sessions with David, he still found it difficult to recognise me because I remember that at lunch time, when some of the mothers collected their children, he would have gone off quite happily with anyone. On one occasion he followed a mother whose coat was the same colour as the one I was wearing at that time. However the sessions were beginning to have some effect. He seemed to be more aware than he had been. It began to dawn on me gradually that he only appeared to understand the word 'shoe' as he would look down at his feet if this word were mentioned. I tried other words but he showed no response. He wasn't deaf. Was it possible not to be deaf and yet not to understand words? The next time I saw the consultant I established that there was indeed such a handicap and that it was known as aphasia. However he assured me that David did not suffer from it.

The consultant noticed quite an improvement in him. I'd had a difficult job getting there, David had been previously on the ordinary tube trains and had learned to accept them, but on this particular line London Transport were still using the old brown wooden electric trains, interspersed with the larger type Metropolitan tubes. The first train to come in was a brown wooden one and David would have nothing to do with it. We let that one go. The next was a Metropolitan line train. I managed to get him on this one, it was more like the smaller tube trains of other lines. David noticed it was larger though and screamed intermittently all the way to the hospital. This time we didn't have to wait long. Waiting with David was always a strain.

I was glad the consultant noticed a difference; it confirmed my own observations. He said that although he had diagnosed David as emotionally disturbed he couldn't rule out the possibility that he was suffering from high tone deafness and made an appointment for him to have his hearing tested again. As well as this I was asked to take him to another hospital for tests. I didn't enjoy these visits. The specialist was psychoanalytically oriented and believed that David's problems arose from his environment. She was particularly interested in interpreting drawings but she couldn't find much to analyse at this stage. David was more likely to throw the crayons across the room than to draw with them. I had to take him on Saturday mornings and first there would be a longish wait in the corridor, which was trying with a child like David, and then, when we were called in to the doctor's room, there would be several other mothers with their children. Compared with David, they seemed to behave quite normally. I was glad when, after a few months, we didn't have to go any more. It took up time and seemed pointless. In fact I found visiting hospitals an absolute nightmare. When David was young he was entirely without any understanding of social situations. He would behave in a really outrageous manner and I would be powerless to stop him. It was especially difficult if I had to take Paul with me and even worse if I was without the support of my husband who could rarely take time off to come with me. Hospitals appear to make block bookings and one may have to wait up to one and a half hours in a room or corridor with other mothers with children who look and behave so normally that one wonders why they are there. The other mothers would stare at David and I could almost hear them muttering 'spoilt brat' under their breath. David wouldn't look at the toys provided for his amusement but was likely, if he got the opportunity, to dash into side wards to rifle cupboards and drawers in search of metal objects, or to tip up any handbag within reach.

It happened several times that when at last we were called in to the interviewing room we were confronted by a complete stranger. Usually he would appear not to know anything about David. In spite of the large dossier of case notes in front of him he would ask for David's name and date of birth and I would have to give his history right from the beginning. Then we would go home. After all, he wouldn't be aware of any change in David's behaviour as he'd never seem him before and he probably knew nothing about autism anyway. I wouldn't ask any questions as he wouldn't know the background nor would he be likely to see David again. It meant that a difficult journey and an unpleasant wait had been for nothing and, moreover, David would not see the specialist for twelve months—which can seem a long time when one needs reassurance.

Some doctors are very kind and considerate. Some are distant, some seem to consider you are without feelings as they will talk about your child as if he's disposable—one of nature's mistakes—and that you can forget all about him and start again.

Most of the doctors I met were, fortunately, in the first category, though I experienced some harrowing times while waiting to see them. There must be ways, surely of devising a proper appointment system.

And meanwhile I found out all I could about aphasia. It seemed that there were two kinds; expressive and receptive. Children with receptive aphasia could hear words but were unable to understand what they meant and were therefore unable to speak. Children with expressive aphasia could understand what was said but were unable to speak. The condition was uncommon and most children though suffering from one form of the handicap yet had a degree of the other. It seemed to me that David *must* have a receptive aphasia and that his problems arose from his lack of understanding of language and not lack of language from emotional disturbance. When he went for his hearing test I mentioned this, as it seemed that he was not deaf in any way. I demonstrated that if I took off his woolly hat and said 'Pick it up' he took no notice but if I made him look at me and then pointed to the hat, he would pick it up. The audiologist had been inclined to pooh pooh the idea but after this little demonstration he wasn't so sure and gave me the name of the leading specialist in this field. It was true that with David gestures had to be over-emphasised. Paul for instance could read meaning into the twitch of an eyebrow or the lifting of a shoulder.

When I went back to the consultant I asked if it were possible that David suffered from aphasia and added that I should like to see the specialist in this field. The Consultant didn't think this likely and dissuaded me and I let it rest. All the same it gave me ideas and once I'd gained David's attention at our evening sessions, I began to name common household objects such as 'chair' 'table' 'mug' 'spoon' and so

on. To my delight he learned these easily and even generalised quite well. He realised that a chair was something one
sat on and I didn't have to show and name every chair in the
house. I found later that this was unusual. At about the same
time I began to show him pictures of these objects and found
that he could recognise them. The Sister at the school had
also found the same thing. It seemed that if he were shown
one thing at a time and its name was clearly given he would
not forget it. It was apparent that his memory was good and
that he could be taught.

It was around this time that I had an odd experience. I
dreamed that I was only about three feet tall. I could judge
this because the ground was so close. When I looked down I
could see that I was wearing David's yellow mackintosh and
wellingtons and I was running along the kerbside, jumping
on the grilles of the drains, just as he did. Suddenly one gave
way and I felt myself falling into blackness. Just at this point
I woke to hear David screaming. I ran into his room telling
him over and over again that he hadn't fallen down the
drain, until he fell asleep.

Just after David had started school I was asked to take
him to see the educational psychologist. After watching him
for a while he said that it was hopeless. David would not get
better and that attempting to teach him was a waste of time.
He said that I would soon find him impossible to manage
and that he'd have to go into a mental subnormality
hospital. He went on in this vein for quite some time. I tried
not to let it worry me but my eyes were blurred with tears
when we left and we were almost run over by a bus because I
stepped off the pavement without looking. It seems odd that
a person who has received training in psychology can lack
understanding of what it must feel like to be on the receiving
end of his remarks.

On the whole I was fortunate that I wasn't inundated with
visits from health visitors or social workers. Except for a few
welcome exceptions, social workers too, in the 1950's, could
be very unfeeling. If they had heard of autism they would
almost certainly have read the current theory that the

handicap was caused by the parents and so would feel
justified in criticising everything the parents did, without
any real knowledge of the handicap or any understanding of
the problems it created. Parents already bewildered and
lacking in confidence were further burdened by being
blamed for the condition. Many visits ended with parents in
tears as I found out later from other parents. I had only one
visit when David was young, apart from the usual one when
we came out of hospital after his birth, and on this occasion I
was told how cleverly Mrs. Brown managed her
handicapped child. I felt the implication was that I wasn't
managing cleverly but apart from that I was left alone. I
needed support but I was now getting all I needed at David's
school.

Every day when I went to fetch him I would see the Sister
who always talked to me. It made us very late home and I'm
sure the Sister often had a very short lunch hour but it was
wonderful to speak to someone who, while realising the
seriousness of the handicap, was encouraging and kind. I'm
sure she gave David far more than his fair share of attention.
There were more than twenty children in the kindergarten
but she obviously spent some time alone with him each
morning. David would amuse himself with the Montessori
equipment but he wouldn't sit quietly while a story was
read. Fortunately the class was arranged so that the children
were free to move around and play with the equipment,
although the teaching was formal. I realised how lucky I
was. Even the nursery school that Paul attended would not
have taken him and I couldn't see any primary school
accepting him when he reached school age unless he
changed radically.

David was not toilet trained. Although only once did he
dirty himself at school I was never sure whether this was just
good timing or whether he really had some bowel control.
However he seemed unable to stay dry for more than half
an hour. We managed with thick towelling pilches and
extra large plastic pants. We carried on in this way until
he was six when he became dry during the day very sud-

denly and dry at night almost immediately afterwards.

Paul and David were very different. Paul at 2½ and David at 4 were still not talking but this is about all that they had in common. David was inactive with sudden bouts of rather aimless overactivity such as bouncing on the sofa in the playroom or running up and down the hall. Paul was always active and he came home from the nursery full of energy after his midday rest. During the light summer evenings he had no intention of sleeping and he made sure that David didn't either. Paul would climb. He was very sure footed and unafraid of heights. David was frightened of falling and liked to stay near the ground. Paul was slim, mercurial and full of mischief. David was solidly built, unadventurous and solemn. David's characteristics may have been due partly to his handicap but I am sure that if Paul had been autistic the condition would have manifested itself very differently.

It was Paul who organised the mischief they both got into. We decorated the small front bedroom using a heavy quality paper and along the top we put a frieze of zoo animals. Then we carefully painted the paper with a colourless liquid designed to repel dirty finger marks. The next morning there was very little of it left, just a few shreds clinging to the wall. Paul would start these little enterprises and encourage David to join in. Paul would know it was wrong, David wouldn't. Having David for a brother had some advantages and Paul was never slow to exploit a situation. He would throw one toy out of the window and get David to throw the rest. Paul would then stand back and await developments. It would have been easier if Paul had been the elder. It was difficult to discipline him when his older brother was allowed to get away with things and at 2½ Paul was not old enough to understand that David was handicapped. At this stage there was a continual clearing up. As fast as I packed up or cleaned one corner they were both making a mess somewhere else.

Just after he was four David began to improve. He could recognise me again. He knew the names of a few household articles and daily he was becoming more aware. I tried to

make him feed himself as he was still using his fingers. It was
surprising how neatly he ate without a spoon but of course he
couldn't go on like this. He held the spoon correctly, would
put food on it, lift it and then just as it reached his mouth he
would turn it over so that the food dropped off. This hardly
encouraged him to continue trying. Every lunch time I stood
behind him, holding his hand with the spoon in it and guided
it to his mouth. It was worth the effort for after a short while
he was feeding himself.

Just before he was 4½ he began to try to talk. He seldom
tried to use speech for communication but would attempt to
copy me. The words were almost unrecognisable and his
voice had an odd flat quality as if he were deaf. It was about
this time that the Sister decided to teach him the alphabet.
She told me what she was doing and I did the same at home.
I didn't know that she was teaching the small lower case
letters and I taught him capitals. At the end of the week he
knew both—and he was not confused. This wasn't so
surprising as it sounds in view of his longstanding interest in
letters. I don't know why I hadn't thought of teaching him
the alphabet before. During one lesson he was the only child
who could name the letter 'm' and Sister said he seemed to
come alive, he was so pleased with himself. Some time
previously I had shown and sounded out the letters on the
little plastic tablecloth which among other things was
decorated with the alphabet. He loved me to do this. I don't
know what it was about letters that he found so attractive. I
doubt if we really taught him the alphabet, I have a
suspicion that he already knew it.

Around this time I took David to see the consultant
again. He was delighted at the way he was getting on which
was really becoming obvious to everyone. I asked once more
if I could take him to see the specialist in aphasia and I was
told once more that he was a very important man and I
mustn't worry him.

As David had learned the alphabet so quickly, Sister
decided to teach him to read and we started off on two and
three letter words which were spelt phonetically such as 'in'

'on' 'cat' and 'mug'. For about a week he didn't see what we were trying to show him and then he caught on very quickly. The biggest benefit was that the words he read were clearly pronounced. Since then he has spoken clearly, though his voice has remained monotonous. Not only is it monotonous its inclined to be too loud and if asked to speak more quietly he goes to the other extreme and whispers. He has always, since he started speaking, had difficulty with pronouns. He didn't suffer from echolalia to any great extent but pronouns confuse him as they keep changing. In time he learned to use 'he' 'you' 'she' and 'I' quite well though he still makes occasional mistakes, but more sophisticated pronouns such as 'ours', 'theirs' 'we' and 'us' were and are very difficult for him.

David learned to read when he was about 4½. At five he was well ahead of most children. He had little difficulty with words that were not phonetic although he didn't understand what they meant. His reading was purely mechanical. He could get no satisfaction from reading a story as he could not understand what it was about. By now he had quite a large vocabulary, but all the words he knew were nouns as these were the things that we were able to show most easily.

It was time to see the consultant again and at this visit he said *yes* I could see the specialist in aphasia as I so obviously would not be happy until I did, though he warned me that it would be a waste of time. An appointment was fixed remarkably quickly and off we went to yet another hospital. I had to take David for three days running for various tests and this took some organising. The first day he was given an IQ test (on the performance scale only, that is, he wasn't tested on his comprehension of speech, which was virtually nil). His performance IQ was found to be well above average. The next day, he was given a rather complicated hearing test. I didn't think he would be able to do it as it involved opening little doors for some sort of visual reward when he could hear the noise. He lost interest towards the end but by that time they had discovered that if he were slightly deaf, which they thought unlikely, it wasn't enough to account for his lack of comprehension of speech. On the last day I saw the specialist who went carefully through his history and said that in his opinion David was suffering from a receptive aphasia, though he preferred to call it congenital auditory imperception. He told me that it was a rare condition and that only one child (with a normal IQ) in 38,000 suffered from it. He asked me to continue as we were doing and to return in 6 months time.

CHAPTER FIVE

Holidays

We had our first holiday with the children in Dorset when David was 2½. We rented a caravan and my husband didn't enjoy it at all. He would have much preferred to stay at home. I knew he wouldn't want to go again, yet I needed to get away from the house for a change of scene. At 3½ David was at his worst. We couldn't have stayed at an hotel even if we could have afforded to. My mother had a cousin living on the south west coast who was an enthusiastic model engineer. As this was my husband's hobby I knew that they would have a lot in common so I wrote to him explaining our difficulties with David and asking if he knew of anywhere we could stay, mentioning that my husband was not keen on caravans. My mother's cousin had lived in the area for years and knew nearly everyone. The small town was even smaller then than it is now. He gave us the address of someone who would let us have two bedrooms and the use of a room downstairs each evening and would supply us with an evening meal and breakfast. We would have to go out each day until dinner time at 7 p.m. On Sundays we would be given a mid-day meal and a light supper.

That September, we travelled by night, arriving in the early morning. It was a beautiful day. The area was very quiet and unspoilt in those days and my husband loved it from the moment we arrived. The landlady was understanding about David and we stayed out all day quite happily with a picnic lunch. If it rained hard we had to stay in the car but otherwise, in drizzle or high wind we wrapped up well and walked as far as we could. We had a fold up pushchair big enough for both of them if need be. After this successful holiday I couldn't get my husband to consider going anywhere else.

In 1957, on our third consecutive holiday in the same place my husband disappeared early on our second morning and came back with an estate agent's list of cottages for sale. Holiday accommodation of the sort we were enjoying was disappearing and David was still not ready to stay at an hotel or guest house. Just before Paul was born an uncle of my husband's had died, leaving us a little money which we had invested. My husband now intended to sell some shares and buy a cottage. This would solve the problem of where to stay once and for all.

This was the wettest holiday we ever spent. It rained for part of every day, sometimes all day. It was fortunate that we had something positive to do. Looking at cottages took up most of our time. We wanted one near the town we had been staying in but couldn't find one that was suitable. Most of the local people preferred new houses so that cottages were extraordinarily cheap and there were a lot of them on the market. We wanted one with main drainage but many of the villages in the area we had in mind were not at that time connected to the main sewer and if the gardens were small, sloped the wrong way or had a stream running through them then the local authority would not allow a septic tank. In the end we found the cottage we were looking for advertised in the local paper. It was smaller than most we'd seen but it had electricity, mains water and main drainage. It was in a pleasant but not particularly pretty village about three miles from the sea.

For years not only did we spend two or three weeks in the summer there, but also two weeks at Christmas and Easter. The only disadvantage was that I exchanged one sink for another. It would have been a pleasure not to have had to cook a meal; to have gone out once in a while to a restaurant without David but this was impossible of course.

Although both children were healthy both had minor weaknesses. At one stage, when David was about two he would worry me by becoming very pale after his midday meal. However, he would look quite healthy and pink in the morning and again in the evening. He was not actually ill and I never discovered what it was that troubled him. He had few tummy upsets apart from occasional travel sickness but he caught a lot of colds. In fact he would catch a cold in October which seemed to last, because of heavy catarrh, until May. But my worst worry was his cough. My poor GP must have been tired of seeing and reassuring me. I knew as well as she did that although it sounded ominous, it meant very little. I come from a family of tickling throats and know that once I have had a cold, I can have an irritable throat for a long time after and cough quite alarmingly. It wasn't really me she had to convince. It was my friends. As soon as they heard him they were sure that he had whooping cough. David, in their eyes, must have had whooping cough every winter for years. When he was four or five I remember asking my GP to write a note saying that his cough was not infectious so that I could take it to his school. I felt very self-conscious but there was little I could do and it was important that he didn't stay at home when he was making such good progress. My doctor told me that I might have to put up with this until he was seven when it was likely that it would disappear. She was absolutely right. It did. Fortunately David did not get bronchitis, though he and Paul had occasional attacks of croup. Croup sounded very different from his other cough and it was obvious that it had to be taken seriously. A few days at home, with a steam kettle, usually cured this. After he was seven, David gave no further cause for concern. Sometimes he looked a little pale, but I never found a reason. Now that he is in his twenties, he would probably be travel sick if we were to take him on a long coach journey or on a very rough sea but he can travel by car without problems.

Paul was a smaller, daintier child than David. He was the picture of health as a baby and a young child. However after he was two he began to have recurrent attacks of tonsilitis and sickness. He seemed to have difficulty in digesting anything rich such as cream, butter or chocolate. Even when kept off these foods he had a bilious attack about once a month and if he went to a party and ate any rich food he was sick most of the following night. The doctor told me that he would get over both the tonsilitis and the sickness by the time he was seven and it is true that he became gradually better after this age although he was twelve before he finally overcame these problems. Paul didn't suffer the same number of coughs and colds as David, nor was he ever travel sick.

David had infantile eczema as a baby and for a little while I had to wash him with oil instead of bathing him. On the suggestion of a friend, I made him cotton mittens to stop him scratching himself as I once found him covered in blood—an alarming experience. But this cleared up after a short while. He had one small reoccurrence when he was about seven but it didn't last. Paul, on the other hand, didn't show any signs of eczema until he was two years old, but once it started, it lasted on and off until he was about eleven when he began to get hay fever. He gave us a horrible fright one day. He came home with a swollen, moonlike face, his eyes had almost disappeared, he'd lost his voice and he'd come out in huge spots. He had only been in the field a few minutes. Usually nothing as dramatic as this happens, he just sniffles and sneezes his way from the end of May until the middle of July. For several years he had a course of injections during the winter. I don't know how much difference this made. He prefers not to take drugs now as they make him feel dopy.

Both children caught the usual childhood illnesses and they posed no particular problem. Both David and Paul had a rash several months apart, that could have been german measles, the doctor couldn't be certain in either case. Whatever it was they could not have caught it from each other as there was too long a gap in between. A year or so after this, Paul caught 'proper' german measles and both David and I caught it from him. They both had measles quite severely and chicken pox. David had mumps but Paul didn't although they shared a bedroom.

We were lucky, I found, that we lived in a middle class area. Most of our neighbours had some understanding of the difficulties of rearing a handicapped child and were on the whole not prejudiced. Nor did they have any of the peculiar ideas I sometimes met when mixing in the wider world. People were not purposely unkind, just rather ignorant so that though their remarks could hurt, one realised that they were without malice and were therefore easy to forgive. In these circles I found that anything Paul did was attributed to having David as a brother—falling off his bicycle was apparently due to having a fit (though neither of them suffer from epilepsy). One parent warned her child to keep away from Paul when he picked up a stick as he 'might be dangerous'. We were told once that David looked wild as his 'hair stood on end'. I can only conclude that he hadn't brushed it that morning.

When we realised that David had some form of mental handicap, we joined the Society for Mentally Handicapped Children (then called the Society for Parents of Backward Children) hoping to meet other parents with similar problems. We went to a number of meetings but we didn't find anyone whose child resembled David in any way. Moreover, at that time David was not aware of other people and behaved very strangely so that the outings and parties that the group put on were useless as far as we were concerned. All the same I remained a member and am one to this day. Later on David was able to take advantage of some of the outings and as time passed I met the occasional parent with a similar problem. This Society is an excellent one for those who have a young child with Down's syndrome or a child who is backward but socially aware. But young autistic children behave very oddly and their parents feel almost as self-conscious at these outings and parties as they do in the outside world. The other parents, unless they too have children who have autistic symptoms, are only slightly more likely to understand their worries and fears than the parents of normal children.

CHAPTER SIX

Five Plus

Now that he was five David began to improve rapidly and we felt as if a load or at least half a load had been lifted from our shoulders. Not only was David improving but Paul was talking. We began to feel more like a normal family. As David could now read, Sister began to teach him to count using the Montessori equipment and I did the same at home with beads and buttons. We counted the beads and wrote the figures down. David loved this and learned very quickly. He found numbers easier to understand than words because they are consistent. Different words can mean the same thing (dish, plate) and words sounding the same can have different meanings (pear, pair). Speech to a child with no ability for its interpretation is confusing. Also we had to make sure that we used the same phrase for the same thing. At first we had to shorten our sentences, cutting out every unnecessary word if we wanted him to understand anything at all. I had been teaching him verbs by acting the more common ones, such as hopping, sitting, walking, sleeping, eating, drinking. He learned these with little trouble, in fact, anything which could be shown presented no difficulty. Talking to David at this stage meant using a noun and a verb so that sentences were, indeed, short. If one talked too fast or used words he didn't know, then he shut off and stopped listening.

He used his first 'sentence' just before he was five. We were looking through a magazine when he saw a picture of a dog being given a bath and said 'dog bath'. He would now respond very well on a one-to-one basis but as soon as I left him to join the wider family circle he lapsed into isolation once more.

At five, the age that children must enter school, the local

authority acknowledged his existence by asking me to take him for an IQ test at the clinic. In 1957 mentally handicapped children were sorted into those who were considered 'educable' that is, those with an IQ of 50 or above and 'ineducable' those who had an IQ below 50. In theory this sounds simple, in practice it is rough justice and the law has now been changed so that this 'sorting' no longer occurs. The children who were thought to be 'ineducable' were sent to Junior Training Centres which were administered by the health department and those with IQ's of 50 and above were sent to a variety of places including schools for the educationally subnormal (ESN) which are and were the responsibility of the education department. Neither Junior Training Centres nor ESN schools were necessarily suitable for autistic children although I know of children who have done well in both.

The then Junior Training Centres and schools for the educationally subnormal were both quite understandably geared to training and teaching the child with some social awareness, who was backward educationally and sometimes physically as well and they were adequately staffed for this purpose. On the whole autistic children do not fit into this pattern and are either so disruptive that many of the schools or centres cannot cope or so withdrawn that they spend the whole day on their own, learning nothing.

The IQ test was in two parts. One part was involved the comprehension of language and the other part tested reasoning ability by the solving of puzzles and was designed to test intelligence not dependent on language. Since puzzles were David's strong point I didn't fear on that score, but I knew that he would never pass the language test. Fortunately I had kept in touch with the clinic doctor who knew that he had a language handicap so that she did not even test him on this but went straight on to the performance test. This consisted of a form board—a board with differently shaped holes into which appropriately shaped pieces had to be fitted. David did this at the speed of light. He also had to assemble a man from pieces consisting of head, body,

right arm, left arm, left and right leg. He took a little longer
over this as he had the right and left leg reversed, but noticed
his error and corrected it. He had passed.

It was at this time that he showed an interest in things that
seemed to have 'magical' qualities. He was fascinated by
magnets and magnifying glasses and would spend hours
absorbed in testing them on objects. He liked making
shadows with his hands, first near the light and then further
away. Later on he loved to play with a gyroscope. It was
difficult for him to see how these things worked, hence their
fascination I think.

It was when David was five and we were on holiday that
he started his running away phase. Fortunately it didn't last
long. We would no sooner sit down on the beach than he
would be off. Our favourite beaches were those with no-one
on them and with plenty of room. This had the advantage
that David could not disturb others by rifling their bags or
picnic baskets nor could he walk right through sandcastles
or beach games without, apparently, noticing them. But the
emptiness gave plenty of scope for running and run he would
until he was a dot in the distance and one of us had to get up
and chase him to bring him back. At least he didn't attempt
to walk into the sea with all his clothes on as he had two years
previously.

The staff at the nursery were delighted that Paul was talking normally and told me what a bright and very normal little
boy he was and David was making fast progress with two of
the three 'R's'. It was hard work getting him to write; he
made faint quavering marks like an old man. When he had
started to go to school his hands had seemed limp and
useless. If asked to hang up his coat it appeared that his wrist
was just not strong enough to lift it to the peg. Having seen
him bend tins and our pewter coffee pot it was obvious that
there was no real lack of strength. It seemed that he was
unable or unwilling to do things which had no meaning for
him.

But now Sister reported that David was doing more for
himself and was daily more aware of the other children.

However, it was still difficult to get him to join group activities or to sit and listen quietly to a story. He was not allowed to take a tin to school and he had to be frisked while he was there to make sure he hadn't managed to get hold of one, although he was allowed to wander round the playground at break, picking up hair grips. At home I discouraged the collection of tins as far as possible as too much concentration on them stopped him from learning other things, but I have never been able to eradicate this obsession and it continues unabated. For short spells he developed other obsessions, but these were short lived, comparatively speaking. We had to watch for their development and to stamp on them quickly before they took hold. Once they had become established we just had to live with them until they wore off. For instance, I was once late in getting his hair cut and he did not like the feel of it on his forehead. He developed a way of shaking his head which continued long after his hair had been attended to, for several months in fact.

Many autistic children are 'spinners', that is, they make to twirl themselves or objects and they can sometimes make the most unlikely objects spin. David liked to watch a record on a record player revolve and he liked his musical top, but otherwise he showed no particular interest. Some autistic children like to dangle a piece of string or carry a stick that they can twiddle. Again David had no desire to do this, nor did he flick or wave his fingers beside his face meanwhile watching from the corner of his eye, another common characteristic. However, he flapped his hands and jumped up and down when he was excited and would also run along with arms flapping. When he was unhappy or frustrated he would bite the back of his hand. He often giggled to himself for no apparent reason. This, again, is not uncommon and it was thought at one time that the child was having hallucinations. If, however, you can get him to tell you why he is giggling it is usually over something quite ordinary although perhaps not a thing a normal person would find amusing. David once told me that he was laughing because two of his tins would look funny stuck together with treacle.

David was now taking to arithmetic like a duck to water.
He learned his tables with the other children and because of
the Montessori equipment and our sessions with the beads
and buttons at home, understood what they were about. He
learned them easily and was very proud of his progress. If
he'd shown any difficulty or distress in learning either
reading or arithmetic then it would have been wiser not to
push him but as these were the things he found easiest to do,
we taught him. It was necessary for him to have some sense
of achievement. I helped him to write but he didn't like it so
we didn't pursue this far. These days he writes, when he has
to, in a childish script. He does not read for pleasure but uses
this skill for notices, signs, for finding out about radio or
television programmes or for following directions on tins and
packets. Arithmetic is useful in daily life too. He can do
square roots in his head but this does not appear to have a
practical application, so he uses his ability for shopping. He
can calculate his change and he does not try to spend more
money than he has. At six years old it was impossible to
know what he would be like when he was grown up so that
we felt that the more skills he could learn the better equipped
he would be.

His most profound problem is language comprehension.
There are a few autistic children who have not had David's
intelligence and who have progressed more than he because
they have been better able to communicate. Though
autistic, they may not have shown any marked islets of
intelligence but have yet been able to speak more readily and
grammatically. We all worked hard at trying to teach David
to understand language and we tried never to let an
opportunity pass for explaining the meaning of a word when
a set of circumstances arose which made the meaning
apparent. As he was bright he would pick up the sense if it
were made obvious enough, but abstract words really posed
an enormous problem and one that we've never properly
overcome.

I was now taking David to see two consultants. I saw each

of them every six months which meant a trip to London every three months. I was told that this was most unusual. We were fortunate that both agreed to this arrangement. We were even told that they had had an amicable disagreement over his handicap at some dinner party. In those days most specialists thought that autism was an emotional disturbance caused by the child's parents or by his general environment. Autism was found more frequently in middle class or intellectual families and it was believed that these parents provided a cold unstimulating home life. I had a kind consultant who never actually accused me or my husband of coldness, but I thought that some of the questions I was asked were odd. The same interest would surely not have been shown in the habits of the parents or in the home environment of spastic, deaf or blind children.

Now that David was over six years old, the specialist in aphasia asked me who was paying his school fees. When he found out that we were, he wrote to our local authority and shortly afterwards we had a letter from them saying that they would be paying in future. I must say here, that although our local authority had not taken responsibility for David's fee earlier, once they did become involved they were wonderful. There was never any hint that financial backing would be withdrawn. Indeed, if I had any problem over education, I knew I could visit the education officer or his assistant and be assured of support. In all ways, life was getting easier. It was around this time, just before David was six, that I passed my driving test. A small thing perhaps, but one that in my case, made an enormous difference to my life. I could get to school in seven minutes instead of the three quarters of an hour it had been taking.

Because the local authority was now paying the fees, the educational psychologist who had so upset me two years previously, was sent to the school to give official approval. When I went to collect David at lunch time I was met by the Principal who was most indignant. The psychologist, after watching David, had said that it was no wonder he behaved as he did as he had an unstable mother. He then recounted

how upset I'd been when he'd seen me. The Principal asked
him if he had any children (apparently he hadn't) and
suggested that he, too, might have been upset under the
same circumstances. She also said that she considered me
one of the most stable of mothers. I could have hugged her.

It was while we were furnishing our cottage that David
had lunch at school once a fortnight. There was an auction
every other Tuesday at the local auction rooms and over the
next six months I gradually acquired most of the furniture
we would need for it. This was the first step towards David
staying at school for a longer period. Once I had all the
furniture, he continued to stay on Tuesdays, in fact he stayed
every Tuesday. Now that he was toilet trained there was no
problem.

Seven

At seven years old, David was getting on rather well, considering the severity of his handicap. Looking back it seems the years between six and a half and eight and a half were probably his happiest and most encouraging. He was learning words fast. I taught him adjectives and opposites; long/short, big/little, fat/thin and adverbs, quickly, slowly, quietly. The prepositions that could be demonstrated were also easy to teach; on, off, under, over, beside, behind. He knew colours and could name them all, even colours such as beige and cream. He began to understand simple conversation if it was aimed directly at him. His spelling was accurate and he loved arithmetic and music.

When he was seven the Principal told me that he would be leaving the Montessori class and going into the main school with the others of his age. The previous year the policy of the Convent had changed and boys, like girls, could now stay until eleven years old. This was wonderful news for us as it meant that we didn't have to look for anywhere else just yet. He left the Sister who had been so good to him and went into a class of boys only, with a master.

David made the change quite well, though he reverted to wetting his bed for a few weeks. During this time I gave him a tin every time his bed was dry and he was soon all right again, though this was probably because he quickly became used to his new form and got on well. He wet himself once at school because he didn't know how to ask to be excused. Sister had taken care of him previously. I suggested that the master ask one of the boys to take him to the cloakroom at break and after a few days he went on his own. David was now staying two full days a week; Tuesdays and Thursdays.

The specialist thought that speech therapy might help so

that it was arranged that David should go to the local clinic. The school he was attending was not in our own borough and the specialist contrived that he should attend speech therapy in the same borough as his school which made things easier. I could collect him from the Convent and go straight there. At this time there were few concrete nouns and verbs that he did not know but he still could not hold a proper conversation. He couldn't understand such words as 'if', 'unless', 'until'—in fact, the abstract but very necessary words. He frequently misunderstood me and he would often ask me to sing what I had to say as for some reason he found this easier to understand. He asked me what the words 'the' and 'and' meant. Language just didn't come naturally. On the other hand, he liked to make up words. He called a red jumper he was very fond of, his red 'trip', and thought this very funny.

The speech therapist did not know anything about aphasia and told me that she couldn't find a word that he didn't know. It transpired that she was testing him on nouns and I tried to explain that, on the whole, he didn't have problems with these, but she never really understood. Fortunately the students who were employed there did. They had been trained to help people who had had strokes. David had trouble with words such as 'how', 'which', 'what', 'why', 'who', 'when', 'where' and he was given exercises to try to help him. I remember that at this time he would go up to people and say 'What's this?' instead of 'Who is this?' or 'What's your name?' But the hardest word seemed to be 'why'. He would use 'What for' instead. 'What for dig garden?' 'What for go school?' If I wanted him to understand the word 'why' I had to say 'Why do you drink water . . . . because?' and then let him answer. If I did not add the word 'because' he could not understand the question.

Between seven and eight David learned most of the everyday skills which one takes for granted. He learned to dress and undress himself, to use a knife and fork, tie his shoelaces, to wash and bath himself and to clean his teeth. He had no particular difficulty with these things, though they had to be taught rather than just picked up. He was becoming much more civilised and it was possible to take him out with us without feeling that he would behave oddly. He seemed quite normal when he didn't speak. Once he learned a thing it was never forgotten.

Paul on the other hand would know a thing one day and forget it the next. In all things social, Paul left David far behind but at this stage David was academically far in advance of Paul. Paul would get David to read his books to him. Paul couldn't read, but he could understand the story; David could read but didn't know what he was reading. On one occasion Paul was very cross because David read the word 'wind' with a short 'i' instead of a long one. Paul did not understand that words could be spelt the same way yet have a different meaning and pronunciation and David didn't get the gist of the story so didn't know how to pronounce the word.

Although it is said that autistic children do not imitate, I noticed that David usually played with a toy or used a thing correctly once, demonstrating that he knew what is was for, but apart from his educational toys which he would play with in the intended manner, he would then misuse it. This behaviour was similar to the way that he suddenly learned to run and greet me, but had to be reminded to do so and the way he realised what pointing was for and spent the whole of one afternoon pointing to things and then forgot about doing it again, still prefering to lead me by the hand when he wanted to show me something. He would never call me, though he would come if I called him. It seemed that he understood these things, became aware intellectually why they were done and tried them out but never had any inner urge to do them himself.

He would look for tins at every opportunity. He had learned the hard way that he could only have empty ones that would be thrown away. I found that my tins of polish needed replacing rather frequently, and it took me a little while to realise that he was removing some each day so that the day the tin would be empty would be sooner rather than later. He preferred round tins which he could bend in half, forming a rough D. He would draw this shape too and was particularly fond of a curved piece of metal he had found that he called a 'lake'. Later we found this was a Blakey and that these were metal caps which were nailed to the heels of shoes to lessen wear. He had found one on which the B and Y had worn off. He kept his 'lake' for several years. At this time he mostly bent the tins in half and jumped and stamped on them. He would then line them all up and gaze at them. He knew each one individually and where he had found it.

Every Saturday afternoon the children would go to their grandparents who lived just round the corner from us. I was alarmed on one occasion to get a phone call from the police to say that they had David there and would I please go round and collect him. When I arrived at the police station I found David, looking sheepish and obviously aware that he was in trouble, and a very annoyed householder. Apparently she had found him in her garage busily unscrewing the tops of her petrol cans and no doubt bending them up. I explained that he was handicapped and she agreed to take the matter no further. I spoke to the policeman who said that they hadn't noticed that David was handicapped at first but after talking to him for a while they had realised that something was wrong. He had given his name and phone number eventually. Apparently the woman had walked round our road with him and he must have passed our house but didn't say anything; he was no doubt scared of what we would say. When I spoke to him later he said 'policeman say cut arms and legs off and burn David up in bonfire' which I think is most unlikely. Perhaps it is what he thought they'd do.

On another occasion he was brought across the road from the neighbour's opposite. It was plain from the expression on, and indeed the colour of, his face he knew he had done wrong. He had been found rifling through her dustbin looking for tins. It was almost impossible to stop him without locking him up and most people in the road knew him by this time and were tolerant of his behaviour. I sent him upstairs after showing strong disapproval but I knew that it would

only stop him temporarily. In fact it was the first of many
such occasions, the pull of tins was far too great, far greater
than the fear of getting into trouble.

At about this time my sister came to stay for the weekend
and we were to drive to my parents' house on the Sunday. At
that time they were living on the other side of London. I had
prepared a small bag of things to take with us for the day and
had included David's travel pills which were in a little metal
box. I had placed the bag on top of the hall cupboard out of
his reach, but my sister wanting something from the bag,
had taken it down and left it on the settle, not realising why I
put it on the cupboard. I happened to go into the hall and
caught David in the act of helping himself to pills, no doubt
so that he could have the tin. He was able to tell us that he'd
had about five so we dropped everything and dashed round
to the local hospital where they had to use a stomach pump.

The incident of the police and the pills did not seem to
have a great reaction on him at the time but for some while
afterwards I would hear him laughing, a thing he often did
when he was disturbed or unhappy as if to reassure himself,
and found him acting these episodes out. In one case he
mimicked getting into the police car and being driven to the
station and in the other he pretended to put a tube down his
throat.

David had had to go to the casualty department at the
hospital once before. That time he had eaten a Mothak, or
perhaps part of one—we never found out. It was a Saturday
and the doctor couldn't get hold of anyone at the factory to
find out what they were made of. It had no effect on him
fortunately.

Paul was far more accident prone. I had to take him to the
casualty department at 2½ years old when he tripped and
fell downstairs and broke his collar bone, when he cut
himself on glass (twice), when he swallowed a screw, after a
wasp sting on his face and the last time after falling off his
bicycle and fracturing his skull. That time he had to stay in
and was there for three weeks.

When we were staying at the cottage one Easter holiday

my neighbour came round to ask if I knew that Paul was sitting on our thatched roof. I didn't of course. Another time this same neighbour came to tell me that he had started a fire in the little erstwhile privvy at the bottom of the garden. There was no doubt that he could get into mischief when he didn't have anything to occupy his time. Fortunately he began to take an interest in collecting stamps when he was eight years old and this became a serious hobby which took most of his spare time and pocket money for years.

CHAPTER EIGHT

Literal Life

As far as David was concerned our life was becoming easier. He was making rapid progress in all factual subjects. He loved arithmetic and his greatest joy was to be given sums to do. He could read, mechanically, any word and could spell accurately. We could show him places on a map and pictures of past events and this had to pass for geography and history because he did not have enough language to understand these subjects properly. He enjoyed simple science from children's books as a lot could be learned from diagrams and he could follow an illustrated story with a bit of help. He was clever with his hands and with encouragement would have been good at constructing cut-out models. Unfortunately, I wasn't any help to him there.

At eight he was talking much more though far from normally. However, he spoke sensibly and his questions showed that he thought things through. He asked 'Where David come from?' and told me that if he fell down and broke we should buy another David at a David-shop. To help him to understand I had to be careful with irregular verbs I would have to say 'We buyed it' and 'He stealed it'. Conversations of this sort sounded odd and when we were in public people would often turn round and stare. I noticed that he watched people's lips when they were talking as if it would help him to understand better what they were saying. He sometimes appeared to mishear a sentence and would repeat it back wrongly as if querying it. Whenever he heard a new word he would ask us to write it down or if we were out, to spell it. He liked to see each new word written down. Once he had seen it in this form he would never forget it. On one occasion when we were in the car, a piece of agricultural machinery went by, making a squeaking noise. David, who was about seven at the time, leant forward and said 'Looks like a bird'. It took us a few seconds to realise that he meant 'Sounds like a bird' as we'd almost forgotten the machinery. We corrected him and he asked us to spell 'sound' so that he could visualise it. He was inclined to switch the order of words in sentences. For some time he would say 'What that mean word?' instead of 'What does that word mean?'.

David was very literal. He could not understand innuendo nor read people's faces easily. By the time he was seven or eight he knew if people were pleased or angry but was unable to understand the more subtle expressions. Really his only way of interacting with others was through language but his comprehension even on a one to one basis was on a primitive level. If he were asked the classic question 'What would you do if you cut yourself?', he would say 'bleed'. If we said 'What (programme) are you watching?' the answer would be 'television' and if asked 'Where are we?' he would answer 'In the car' instead of naming the town. Once he came with me when I took our cat to the vet. He watched, fascinated, while the syringe was prepared. The vet said that he seemed interested and asked 'What are you going to be when you grow up?' David said 'A man'.

David would make personal remarks in a clear penetrating voice. He'd say 'man got no hair', 'lady got crooked nose' or make other unflattering comments. Later he learned that he mustn't say things of this kind and would make personal remarks in an equally penetrating whisper. On one awful occasion we were sitting in a pullman carriage at a terminus and an extremely large and prosperous woman got in. She took off her furs and sat down, taking up two seats. Stupidly, I was reading and not watching David. When I looked up I realised that I was going to be too late. Before I could distract him he said 'What a big fat lady'. David at that time was eleven years old.

Like most autistic children David learned to say 'no' long before 'yes'. 'No' is so much more positive and its meaning clearer. 'Yes' can leave one wide open to a number of situations. All the same when he grew older he would say 'yes' to almost anything one said apparently in an effort to please rather than to indicate agreement. I decided that I would have to take this in hand and developed some exercises such as 'Do birds fly?', 'Is grass pink?' in an effort to teach him the correct response. When he answered wrongly on one occasion I asked him why. The question had been an extremely simple one and was surprised when he said 'Mummy speak very quietly'.

At eight we had every reason to hope that David would continue to make the rapid progress that he had made over the previous two and half years. One day the Principal came up to me and told me that he had a 'university brain'. Apparently he had sorted out some complicated mathematical problem rapidly and correctly. If he had only been able to make a breakthrough in communication, he would have made fast progress but he was stuck on a very concrete level and each new abstract word or concept was a struggle to acquire though we tried to make use of every opportunity. He asked me how old his teacher was and I said 'perhaps he's 29', 'perhaps he's 31'. 'Don't know, perhaps he's 30'. From this he learned the word 'perhaps'—one of the more useful words. Now we could explain that we might not be going to do a certain thing. '*Perhaps* we'll go for a picnic'— and not get screams of frustration if we didn't go. From 'perhaps' he learned 'might' and 'maybe'. 'If' was more difficult and he often missed its significance. The length of the word was not important. He learned the word 'inaccessible' quite easily as I could demonstrate it and he would use it sometimes to the amazement of other people. Once we forgot his 'break', an apple and I was able to show him that I didn't have it with me and that I'd left it at home. 'Forget' was another useful word and if he became upset over anything I would tell him to 'forget it'. However he puzzled everyone at school because once, when something went wrong there, he, wishing to be reassured said 'forget it'. The teacher kept saying 'no, we won't forget it' only to find that this made matters worse. Fortunately our lines of communication were excellent so that we quickly sorted this out.

David was very aware of his failure and was able to compare himself with others. His teacher told me that he'd asked him who the cleverest boy in the class was, fully expecting him to say 'David' but he said 'Kennedy', who actually *was* the brightest boy. He compared his work with others and would not accept unwarranted praise. I have since been told that this is unusual in autistic children.

He always knew whether people were judging him and would try to do something intelligent to show them that he was really bright. Unfortunately, these actions were not always noticed or their significance was not always seen, so that he would be disappointed. One day, on a visit to the Science Museum he became particularly disturbed when his brightest efforts were not remarked on but he was going through a very disturbed stage at that time anyway. Usually he was philosophical.

The consultant had spoken to a colleague about David and she had professed an interest so I was asked if I'd mind taking him to see her. The consultant told me that it was for her interest only and that she wouldn't be able to help in any way. David must have been about seven at this time. The educational psychologist sat with him with the test material designed for his age level and told me that he'd done extremely well. After this performance test the doctor asked three questions, one of which I've forgotten but the others were 'What would you do if you went out and it was raining?' and 'What would you do if you were late for school?' David could not answer the questions. In the first one the only word he would have understood would have been 'rain' and in the second 'school'. Because he wasn't deaf and although he'd passed his performance test with flying colours she pronounced him severely retarded. When I told the specialist in aphasia this he was angry. Of course we realised that David was severely handicapped and that unless he managed to learn more language he would become retarded, but this was rather a different matter and is almost on a par with calling a deaf child retarded because he cannot hear.

Because of his lack of communication skills David's

behaviour was poor. We were fairly strict with table manners so that we could take him out with us but because of limited comprehension and an inability to understand facial expression and fine gesture he was not very interested in meeting people or aware of what was happening around him. If one knew the limits of his language and could meet him on his own level, then it was surprising how much he could take in but most people would not be aware of this nor would they expect to have to give him their undivided attention. It is not that he is unsociable, in fact he enjoys being with others but he has no idea how to interact with them. I think the most hurtful incidents for me have been those where he has been rebuffed; where he has made an effort to behave normally only to fail. He once joined other children in a group and looked so happy for a short while but without the ability to understand their games, was soon on the outside again. On other occasions he has smiled in expectation of a greeting only to be ignored. He once, after listening to Paul chatting, came into the kitchen and 'chattered' to me. It was gibberish, of course and he realised it. Another time he tried to give up his tins and spent quite some while concocting 'games'. This lasted for two days only and was rather like someone trying to give up smoking. He couldn't get any pleasure and so returned to his tin bending.

At the beginning of the school year when David was eight and a half it was decided that he would not go up a form with the other boys but would be placed in a mixed class of children approximately a year younger than himself. A nun was in charge of this form but not the Sister he knew so well. It was felt that his former classmates would be doing work that would be too abstract for him to follow; there would be more emphasis on subjects such as history and geography and he would be expected to sit quietly and listen. It seemed apparent that he would not learn very much. No one foresaw any problems and for the first few days everything appeared to be going well.

At the end of the first week the Sister asked me if David had toothache. I was quite sure he hadn't. He has excellent teeth, moreover he had just been for a check up. She said that every so often he would put his finger between his teeth and give a short scream. A few days later, when I went to fetch him, he took me by the hand and led me to a formroom and told me that it was for big boys, meaning his former classmates. We were continuing with our usual lessons at home, but suddenly, one evening he became very upset. He broke his pencil in half and screamed and screamed. I couldn't understand what was worrying him at first and then he told me that he had 'no brain' and 'a little forehead'.

I saw the Principal and explained how upset he was and it was decided to let him drift along for a bit. In fact he was now difficult to teach, because when shown anything new he promptly said he had a 'little brain' or that it was 'too difficult' for him. After a while he became less upset but he'd lost all his former interest in learning. When I went up to bed I would go into the bedroom he shared with Paul and would whisper into his ear over and over again 'David is a very clever boy' hoping that this would get through to his subconscious. I don't know whether it made any difference, but in any case I had to give up doing it for, after a while, it began to wake him up.

Although he wasn't taught anything new, the Sister made sure that he didn't forget what he'd learned already. At home I only gave him things that I knew he could do and continued to help him with language and social behaviour. There were no big strides. I explained to him as simply as I could that he had a language handicap. He understood and cried a little.

This year was not a particularly happy one as little progress was made by either child but having the support of the staff at David's school made it easier to bear. In any case we hoped he was marking time before sprinting forward once more.

CHAPTER NINE

Other Parents

On Paul's first day at the convent I was amused to see that David led the way and took great pleasure in showing him where everything was. Now that Paul was with him David was to attend school full time. They were put in the same form and taught by the master who had taught David a year previously. Paul was delighted to have left the school he'd hated but I couldn't say that the was a model pupil. After his failures he did not enjoy being educated, though I never had any more problems with imaginary aches and pains.

One morning for some reason that I cannot now remember, I could not take the children to school. Although they would have to change buses, there were no roads to cross, so I suggested that they went on their own and gave Paul the fares for both of them. I checked with the school and found that they had arrived safely, but it wasn't until they were home again, that I discovered that the journey had not been without incident. Apparently David was so anxious to show Paul he knew which bus to catch, that at the bus station, he'd run from one bus to the other and Paul, who had the fares, had nearly missed it.

Paul still had problems. I was pleased to hear him reading so well but was chastened when, on looking over his shoulder, to find that he read the phrase 'a heap of stones' as 'a pile of pebbles'. I realised that he was still not reading properly, that, in fact, most if it was guesswork, though he could spell words out if he made an effort. I was told that he was mischievous and clowned around but now I was told this kindly, which somehow made a difference.

At home he was well behaved although he was going through a whining phase which lasted for some time. His favourite phrase was 'It's not fair'. Whining is something I have no patience with and I refused to listen telling him that life is seldom fair and why should he expect it to be? I saw him in middle age as the perpetual moaner, always saying that if he'd only had the chance . . . . instead of getting down to at least attempting to remedy things for himself. In this I did him less than justice. Now that he's grown up I don't think I've heard him moan about anything.

Paul wasn't altogether happy to be so closely involved with his handicapped brother. Being at the same school and in the same form, now that I look back on it, may not have been a good idea. All the same, it was far from disastrous and slow progress was made by both children. David learned a few more words. He was still showing resistance to learning new things though not so adamantly as before and a little pressure was exerted. In fact, so long as he wasn't forced unduly he seemed to be quite happy and his murmurings of 'too difficult' were becoming a habit rather than a true expression of his feelings. Now that he was ten we realised that we should have to start looking for another school and this was a real worry. I have often wondered since whether I should have taken the Principal's advice. She suggested that he should go on, with the older boys, to the senior school which was in a city about 12 miles away. There was a train which he could have caught but the station it left from was some distance away. The difficulties of this daily journey seemed enormous to me, though the Principal was certain that he would be able to manage.

It was when David was nine and a half that the first get-together of parents of autistic children took place at the Ambassadors Hotel in London. It was at this meeting that I agreed to go on to a small committee to see what could be done to help and it was through a parent on this committee that I heard of a school in the south east that might take David although it was predominantly a school for normal children. This was useful information which in due course we followed up. Shortly after this I heard a news item on the wireless about a proposed school for children who, though of average intelligence, were unable to speak normally because of 'emotional' difficulties. In our opinion David had 'emotional' difficulties because he was unable to communicate properly. However I realised that this referred to children with the same problems and I contacted the BBC who put me in touch with the organisers of this project.

At around this time David's specialist had arranged for him to go for a week's trial at a special school for children with aphasia. This school was the only one in the country for children of David's age and with this handicap. They were very exacting and few children met their criteria and were accepted. So although places were inadequate for children like David we had a few irons in the fire.

It was during the winter of 1961/62 that parents of autistic children began to mobilise themselves and meetings were held in a parent's house as often as once a week as we decided what we should do. I began leading quite a different life, meeting a wide variety of people, certainly a wider group than I would have met in my rather restricted existence. I enjoyed listening to other better educated parents arguing a point. I realised what I had missed by not going to university. Although our association covered the whole spectrum of society, the early years were made conspicuous by the intelligence of the majority of parents. They were nearly all professional people; doctors, lawyers, university lecturers, architects and they were not overawed by authority. Later, parents from a larger section of society joined us and meeting these parents widened my world even further so that now I feel comfortable with anyone from whatever walk in life. This has been the plus side of having an autistic child.

At this time there were few of us but on the whole we were articulate and determined. The majority of the parents had children far younger than David mostly in the 3–5 years old age group. Autism, in London at least, was at last beginning to be more readily diagnosed. In those days most parents were told that their children were of normal intelligence but were suffering from a psychosis, the implication being that this psychotic condition had been brought about by the parents. Most of the parents were middle class and it was assumed that they were intellectual and had not given the child the love and warmth that he needed for his normal emotional development and that because of this he had retired into his own world to 'escape'. It is only fair to say here that some specialists still believe this to be true (though their numbers are diminishing) and, as no one can yet say how autism is caused, then they cannot be proved wrong. In many ways it is a theory which holds attractions, especially as, if it were true, it is possible to believe that the child can be cured if given enough love.

I remember reading of this theory several years before. I had spoken to the Principal saying that it was all my fault that David was handicapped. I remember how she'd rounded on me quite fiercely, saying that this was rubbish, that no mother would be able to have this effect on a child; that she knew that it had nothing to do with me. I remember that she had pulled me out of a little wallow of self abandon which I was quite enjoying, telling myself how wicked I had been, remembering every little incident; how I'd left him to cry or hadn't run fast enough to help him with something. I recognised then, after speaking to the Principal, something that I had really known all along. David was handicapped, had been born with a handicap and that his major problem was his inability to communicate with others or to understand others when they tried to communicate with him. It has made me all the more determined to press the consultant to allow me to see the specialist in aphasia. To hear other parents talking of 'emotional difficulties' brought it all back very vividly.

At this time I assumed that all autistic children were like David, that is, that they all had normal intelligence, but poor comprehension of language. As in most things in life, nothing is as simple as this. Most autistic children are multiply handicapped and about 75% score below the normal range on a performance test. In fact about 50% are severely subnormal in spite of their normal, even bright and alert expression. David, when young, was only overactive for brief spells, but most are very hyperactive and this poses enormous problems to mothers with other children to look after and homes to run. Apart from the fact that David was less active in his early years, he appeared not to differ greatly from the other children. It was wonderful to meet more parents and to find that I was not alone with my problems, that in fact David was not unique as I had thought. Now with hindsight I think that where David differed from many of the others in his early years was in his 'islets of intelligence'. That is, that in spite of being so isolated he was yet able to recognise and sort colours, letters and shapes, to manipulate small objects and to play with educational toys.

I had met three other parents with similar problems before this, all living in the same borough. One I had only met once. She had a boy who was very withdrawn and who attended a Rudolf Steiner school. Another had a boy, or rather young man (he was eleven years older than David) who was not so seriously handicapped though his handicaps were not the same as David's. He could talk far better and was much more interested in language. He had the same mathematical and musical abilities, though he had very poor co-ordination. For instance, in spite of his use of language ability in maths and music he had never learned nor could he be taught to tie a bow. The other, a girl, was about David's age. She was much more disturbed and not so academically advanced. In those days I wondered whether the children had the same handicap. However, now I was to hear about and meet a much wider range of children and this I found absorbing. I could see the similarities more clearly. It taught me how autistic children vary one from the other, while remaining distinctly 'autistic'.

Autism is a difficult handicap to explain in a few words. Perhaps the simplest definition is that autistic children have great problems in understanding what they see and what they hear in spite of physically normal eyes and ears. What I really didn't grasp for some time, although I lived with and watched David and Paul every day, was that while autistic children, like aphasic children, have difficulties in under-standing language their problem is aggravated by not being able to comprehend facial expression, subtle gesture and bodily stance which also convey meaning and are another more primitive form of language. Speech is surely a 'man made' extension of facial expression, gesture, stance and vocal sounds made by our fellow animals, and it is the instinctive comprehension of all these forms of communication which autistic children lack. Deaf children also have problems in comprehending language but theirs is a physical barrier to sound only. If one can convey language visually, then they are able to understand it. Children suffering from receptive aphasia have problems in interpreting language, though they can hear it but they have less problem with gesture and in understanding facial expressions. Their handicap is severe though not so severe as autism. I knew that before Paul learned to speak that not only did he know what we were saying but that he also watched our faces for every fleeting expression; that he interpreted situations very quickly as much from our expression as from our words. I was aware that David was cut off, I discovered that he did not understand what I said but I did not attach importance at that time to the fact that he did not watch my face; that for a long while he did not look at me. I was only too aware that he was 'withdrawn' but I never considered why, except that the world could have no meaning for him without words. This was an important aspect but not the whole story.

Just before David was ten we were asked to send him for a week's trial to the school for aphasic children. He was to go to the 'cottage' for observation (a small house in the grounds used for this purpose) and we were to take him on Monday and collect him on Friday. David was a little apprehensive when we drove him down. He hadn't been away from us since his stay in hospital when he was three and a half years old but he didn't appear to mind being left when the time came. It seemed odd to be without him at home and we looked forward to fetching him.

We arrived at the school on the Friday afternoon wondering what we should be told but it was as I expected.

Although he had the required IQ on the performance test, his behaviour was thought too odd. However, he had enjoyed his stay and it was reassuring to know that he was not upset at leaving home. One of his fears had been cured too. My husband had made the children a swing when Paul was four or five years old. This swing terrified David. I don't know whether he expected us to grab him and force him on to it but he refused to go anywhere near it which meant that for several years he wouldn't venture to the bottom of the garden. Somehow, the matron or housemother had persuaded him to use the swing at the 'cottage' and he came back with a passion for them. He would go very high, surprisingly considering his fear of heights and would stay on it for far too long, until he turned a pale green in fact.

Another fear that he overcame at about this time, was of a sugar basin. It was an everyday one but he refused to touch it and would back away if it were put near him. Perhaps there was a reason but we never found one. He had never shown much resistance to change, a common characteristic in autistic children. Although he noticed every alteration we made, he didn't seem to mind, nor did he insist on using the same cup or plate as most autistic children do. At this time there were only two things he really minded and one was that the drawer in the kitchen table should be properly shut. If he heard me shut it, he would come all the way downstairs to make sure that it was pushed in just as he liked to see it. The other was car doors. These had to be locked even if we had only just popped out to post a letter. He would have locked the driver's door too, but my husband would not allow this. These were trivial things and not difficult to cope with. Car wing mirrors attracted him for a short while. He had to look in each one and put his tongue out. He also went through a stage of grimacing, this came and went until it eventually stopped altogether. But tins were his main preoccupation and as far as one can tell, always will be. When he was a little older, about thirteen perhaps, he had to murmur 'bus stop' twice every time he saw one as there was usually one on each side of the road, that meant four times, of course. He also had to whisper 'Shell' twice for each Shell pump every time we passed a Shell garage so that there seemed to be a continual sussuration coming from the back of the car.

Now that we knew he wouldn't be going to the school for aphasic children we made an appointment to visit the school in the south east. The headmistress was a charming person and I explained David's problems to her. She had two autistic children at the school, one mildly handicapped and the other more severely affected and she agreed to take him though she warned us that she was no expert. At about the same time we heard from the school which was to take children with 'emotional' problems, asking us to go, with David, for an interview. This school was new, but three children had already been selected and had been under observation at a nearby unit. David was apparently considered suitable without this period of observation and was offered a place.

We now had to make up our minds what to do. In the end, we decided to send him to the school for speech handicapped children with emotional problems. We shall never know whether we made the right decision.

CHAPTER TEN

Special School

David did not go back to school at the same time as Paul. He waited until the end of September. The new special school was opening in temporary premises on the south coast and to start with only four children were to be taken. It was expected that there would eventually be twenty one. Two went in the middle of September and David started two weeks later, with another boy.

We had told him as much as we could about the school and he was not the least bit perturbed about leaving home. As soon as we went in through the door he told the teacher that he had a typewriter and asked if he could have it at school. My husband went home in the car but I stayed the night and followed him home, by train, the next day. There was no problem; David never even turned round to say goodbye.

To one who does not understand the basic handicaps of an autistic child this may sound very strange; that a child may take no notice of his mother's departure, but it is only strange if it is assumed that the child understands social communication. An autistic child learns social communication up to a point but it does not come naturally and instinctively to him as it does to a normal child. I remember how pleased I was when a few years earlier he had run towards me in greeting if I had held out my arms but he had learned to do this by watching other children. A normal child does not have to learn, somehow he knows.

This lack of interest in my departure could be explained, I'm sure, in psychoanalytical terms as rejection and even to the layman it would look as if he did not care whether I was there or not. Parents of autistic children become used to this behaviour, upsetting as it is even to the most hardened. In the last few chapters there will be an attempt to explain this behaviour more fully and perhaps the reasons for it.

It was fortunate that the Society for Psychotic Children as it then was, had been formed the previous May. It gave a new purpose to life. I had offered to help, and, in fact, was kept quite busy recording details of the few children we knew, finding out who had diagnosed each child and what schools, if any, the children had been to. If we were to seek help from official sources, then we had to be as well informed as possible. At first, as official policy was discussed, we had a number of meetings. After so many years of being just a housewife and mother these were exciting days indeed.

Once every two weeks I would travel down to the south coast and take David out for the day. At first this was fun as we could sit on the beach as the weather was mild. Later, when winter came, it was more difficult to find things to do. We would go on to the pier, a little café was still open there, but most of the amusement arcades were closed for the winter so we would be reduced to walking around, well wrapped up. For part of the time we would go to the shops. David always liked a trip round Woolworths and we would spend an hour or so in a news theatre watching the cartoons. David could often understand these and would roar with laughter, throwing himself around in his amusement. His laugh was so infectious that he made others laugh with him. All the same it wasn't easy to find enough to do to fill a day. David was content to go back to school at around 5 p.m. and I would make my way home.

It seemed that David was still saying his ritualistic 'too difficult' when presented with work and in any case, it was the policy of the school to overcome his emotional problems, so that although he was able to add, subtract, multiply and divide in thousands and do long multiplication for pleasure it was decided that he should start again from the beginning. He was given beads to count.

He was also given as many tins as he wanted so he was in sheer heaven. It was hoped that by satiating him he would tire of them. But David could never have too many tins, the more he had the more he wanted. I was told that at the weekly meeting the domestic staff complained of the way that he would go into the kitchen and empty rice and flour on to the floor so that he could have the tins. Behaviour that we would never have tolerated at home. It was felt that these meetings were useful for releasing the feelings of the staff as the school had such difficult children to deal with. We couldn't help thinking that the children need not be so difficult; that perhaps the action or the lack of action of the staff encouraged them to behave as they did. But I must admit that David was very happy during the first nine months at this school. He enjoyed his holidays too but didn't mind going back.

The school had a four term a year system instead of the usual three. This had the advantage that he came home fairly frequently and that each holiday was short. Its inconvenience lay in the fact that he and Paul seldom had holidays at the same time although they would overlap on occasion. This made staying at the cottage difficult and also meant that I was seldom without one or other of the children at home. In many ways I was more tied than I had been before. I was glad that the work I was doing for the Society could be done sitting at our dining room table.

It was during David's first summer at school that I realised that something was wrong. On our days out he did not appear to be his normal self and was reluctant to go back to school. When he came home in June he seemed unhappy as the short holiday drew to a close. I talked to the staff in an effort to find out what was troubling him. There were now three boys at the school who were not autistic but who did not talk. They were very unlike the nine autistic children presently at the school. Although they couldn't speak, they understood what was being said and had no difficulty at all in sizing up a situation from circumstancial clues. One boy in particular had it in for David. I didn't know the extent of this at the time, though I realised from remarks made by the staff that these three boys were teasing him and that he was unable to cope. An autistic child makes a wonderful target, especially one like David who has enough awareness to react to teasing by being scared. Teasing would be wasted on the more handicapped boys as they would not be so susceptible, thereby lessening the fun. I had a word with the headmistress, but she felt that David had to learn to look after himself.

It wasn't until our summer holiday that we realised just how bad things were. We had arranged to go to the cottage via the school so that we would collect him. They, of course, had not broken up and would not do so until the end of September.

That holiday was the worst we had ever spent. David was very unhappy and kept biting his hand and screaming. Once when we were walking along, he suddenly, quite without provocation, started hitting and punching me. He seemed beside himself, hardly aware of what he was doing. I guessed that this was because he was disturbed by the bullying that he had been enduring at school and was determined to get him to tell me about it rather than assume that this was the reason. He seemed afraid to talk about it. In fact he and I walked round and round a field for the best part of an hour while I tried to make him say what was troubling him. At last, after I had almost given up hope, he told me that it was Mark who was teasing him. He dreaded going back to school and when we took him we spoke to the headmistress and asked her to see that he and Mark were not left alone together. It appeared though, that the staff were pleased with the progress that Mark was making; it was felt that he was less inhibited than previously.

As David was so unhappy we asked if he could come home more frequently, perhaps every other weekend, and this was agreed to. At least this gave him less time in which to be bullied.

David was pathetically pleased to get home. We wished that we could afford to bring him home every weekend, but it was quite a long way to travel. At first I would take him back on Sunday afternoons but I found this almost unbearable. We would have to go just after lunch and would leave my husband and Paul by the fireside. David was usually quiet until we reached the mainline station then he would either scream or weep big, fat tears which would run down his face and plop to the ground. I found the weeping heart-breaking, harder to put up with than the screaming. The trains on Sunday were so slow and the whole journey was a nightmare. The passengers, too, must have been mystified—not only by his behaviour but the language I had to use in the effort to explain that I should be back in twelve days time to fetch him. After leaving him at the school, I would wait in an empty, dimly lit street for a bus to take me back to the station and home. It was all very depressing. After a few months I asked if I could take him back on Monday morning, even though he would miss a little school time. We started this in the spring.

It was surprising how much difference this made. I suppose on Mondays he would see that we were all going our different ways and he didn't get the feeling that he was being shut out of his own home. He still hated school, but at least he stopped weeping or screaming on his way back. The train was fast too and everything seemed brighter. After leaving him at school, I would catch a local train and spend the rest of the day with my parents who were once more living on the coast.

Meanwhile I was looking round for another school, a day one. We felt that not only was David not making any academic progress, he was more unhappy and therefore more emotionally disturbed than he had ever been. The school had never claimed to be a centre of academic learning but it was meant to help children with emotional disturbances. It may have achieved this with some, but David's emotions were becoming daily more chaotic.

However, we didn't want to take him away from one school only to find that there was nowhere to send him. A school for normal children which would have been a possibility at one time, was now out of the question. He'd dropped right behind in his school work and was also a very disturbed child. Our education authority was sympathetic;

they were paying high fees for him at his present school and
we did not wish to appear ungrateful.

It was at about this time that David developed one of his
major fears, having just overcome a minor one. About two
years previously he had choked when he tried to swallow a
pill with water. He showed no reaction for a week and then
he began to drink water a sip at a time and to chew his food
over and over before he swallowed it. This slowed down his
eating and drinking and was a nuisance, especially if he
came out with us as he took so long to get through a meal.
After a year or so he overcame this. The next fear was much
more serious and we nearly sent him to hospital for
treatment.

It started when he came home for a weekend. He suddenly
arrived at the kitchen door with his pants and trousers
around his ankles and informed us that he was 'stuck'.
Apparently, he was constipated for the first time in his life
and was frightened. We tried to reassure him and he seemed
to understand.

When he came home next I found he was soiling himself.
He seemed to have discovered how to control his bowels so
that they would pass a little at a time, thus ensuring that he
would never be 'stuck' again. This habit was unpopular both
at home and at school and lasted for eighteen months. Just as
we thought that we would never cure him he stopped suddenly and we had no more trouble. David has a memory like
the proverbial elephant's and once something frightens him
it takes him a very long time to forget the incident. Funnily
enough nose bleeds have never scared him, perhaps because
he had had a number from early childhood onwards. It may
be that he takes them for granted.

Much of the unhappiness David suffered could, it seemed
to me, have been avoided if those in charge of him had been
willing to listen to us. This criticism applies not only to the
school but to hospitals and clinics he had attended in the
past. After all, most parents are not stupid and they know
and understand their child better than anyone else is likely
to. So often parents are not asked, or their opinions are

overridden as irrelevant. Many schools have theories as to why the children behave as they do and they strive to make the behaviour of the child fit their theory. Many specialists do this too. Sometimes a mother knows why her child has acquired a habit and would be happy to explain if asked. Sometimes she finds out, perhaps by reading a paper on her child, given by a specialist or member of school staff, of the peculiar theories put forward to explain away some odd habit her child has developed. She knows how it started and probably why and knows that the carefully built up hypothesis is quite wrong—even ridiculous. The thought of a hall full of people listening to nonsense is bad enough but at least it does not harm the child. It is worse when a mother says that her child will become upset if a certain course of action is followed and no notice is taken of her warning. In the end it is she who is left to pick up the pieces.

During the summer of this year, David's school moved to its permanent premises. Although it was now a lot closer, it took just as long to reach as I had to rely on a series of local buses and trains. The journey was cheaper, however, and he was able to come home every weekend. Somehow I never wanted to use the car, there wasn't a simple way to get there and I felt it would be too wearing. At least I could read and let someone else do the work when I went to fetch him and again when I returned home alone on Mondays. David, too, could travel short journeys by bus and rail without discomfort.

David was glad to have only five days at school and the move made him happier for a short while, but during the late summer and autumn he became more and more miserable—and his health was poor. He had a series of very painful boils and looked pale and run down. We had hoped that he would leave at the end of the September term as we had found another school for him, but just as we thought everything was fixed we discovered that he had to work out a term's notice. Because of his unhappiness, his boils and several heavy colds he spent as much time with us as at school this term. But at last it was all over. He was once more at home, a proper member of the family again. It had taken eighteen months to find suitable alternative placement.

CHAPTER ELEVEN

Selling Autism

The school he was to attend was a private one and one that up to a few months previously had taken only young autistic children. Earlier in the year the headmistress telephoned to tell me that she had been asked to take a boy of eleven and if she could take one of eleven why not twelve? I had gone round to my education department and told them of this. I had been in touch with them about David's unhappiness and they were quite willing to help if they were given information on suitable alternatives. We thought he would be able to start in September, but because of having to stay for a term's notice, he eventually started in January 1965.

When he came home after his first day at the new school he sat in a dream. I had a job to get him to eat his tea. It was obvious that he was thinking about and reliving every moment of the day. I rang the headmistress to ask how he got on and she was delighted with him. He'd plunged right back into work again and within a few weeks his hand biting and other signs of disturbance had subsided. In spite of taking a pill, the car, which was provided by the local authority, was making him feel a little sick but after a short while he seemed to get used to it. The journey was quite a long one for a poor traveller. At this point he was still soiling himself. This habit, like all his habits, would take some time to wear off. The headmistress did not reproach me for this behaviour, nor did she complain about the work it made.

The Society was now well established, the early days of struggle for recognition were past and most of us no longer believed that autism was caused by cold intellectual parents. In the early years we were perhaps too sanguine for our children's eventual normality but perhaps this is no bad thing when the child is young. It was partly this belief in our children's latent abilities that gave us the thrust to get off the ground. If we had realised how serious the handicap was I doubt we would have made the same fight and achieved the same impact.

We still had a massive amount to do. We had to sell the word 'autism'. Autism is not an easy handicap to understand. Everyone can put themselves in the place of a blind or deaf person but how does one explain in simple terms seeing but not understanding, hearing but not interpreting the sound? We had to explain that the children could be helped to understand what they saw and what they heard but that this was time consuming and that the children would never be able to do these things intuitively like the rest of us do, quickly and easily without consciously learning how.

We knew that there must be hundreds of undiagnosed children in the country; that although children living in or near London would probably be recognised, there were many areas where autism would not be diagnosed. Our membership bore this out. Most of them, at this time, lived in or near London and we had clusters of children in some areas and blank spaces in other parts of the country. The numbers of autistic children depended on the specialists who were able to recognise the handicap. We also found that in some places specialists refused to acknowledge that such a condition existed. This was harder. We felt that it might take time to get the handicap recognised throughout the country but it would be very difficult to change attitudes, to make doctors who were unwilling to label children, label them, to make those who did not believe there was such a handicap believe there was. There were also many psychiatrists, probably the majority, who at this time believed that autism was caused by the parents.

Two or three years before we had changed the name of the Society from the Society for Psychotic Children to the Society for Autistic Children (and shortly afterwards to the National Society for Autistic Children). But the word 'autistic' though more suitable than the word 'psychotic' (which has unpleasant connotations, especially for the layman) means 'withdrawn' and a child who is very shy can, in fact, be correctly diagnosed as autistic. (The word 'autistic' had been used to describe these children 20 years previously by the American psychiatrist Leo Kanner, but it was not then commonly used in this country). We had to bend this word, as we could think of no better one, to mean the kind of child we had in mind. A child who was isolated from others by his incomprehension of things seen and heard, by his ritualistic and obsessional behaviour, his odd fears or lack of appropriate fear, resistance to change, lack of eye to eye gaze, odd movements, erratic patterns of eating, drinking and sleeping, abnormal responses to sensory experiences, lack of imaginative play, bizarre behaviour . . . . and yet with all this a bright, alert appearance, quick movements and apparent intelligence in some areas. These 'islets of intelligence' as they have become known, are almost always in the same spheres. Many autistic children show a very early interest in music, some are clever with educational toys or have good constructional or mechanical skills, some have exceptional memories (nearly all autistic children seem to have *good* memories) and others may be unusually quick at mathematics. The M's, in fact—mechanical or manipulative ability, musical or mathematical skill or an exceptional memory. Some autistic children are good at art, some drawing in perspective at a very young age. The more handicapped child does not always exhibit these 'islets'. However, his odd movements such as spinning either himself or objects, flapping his hands or waving them near his face, obsessive behaviour and complete lack of interaction with others will still make him stand out from children suffering from other mental handicaps.

As most of our committee members were articulate and professional people we were fortunate in having within our own ranks the skills we needed for making ourselves known. We also had committee members who, in their own right, were qualified to argue with the psychiatrists who disagreed with our views. Our formation into a registered charity and all legal matters which were and are numerous were dealt

with by another member of the committee. In spite of the
fact that there are relatively few autistic children, we have
made an impact out of all proportion to our size mainly
because, I believe, of the quality of our Executive Committee
which, at the beginning, was composed entirely of parents.

In 1961, at our early meetings before the Society was
registered as a charity, we decided that the most helpful and
most important objectives must be to provide schooling for
the children. At that time there was nothing for them. We
were then talking about infant or pre-school provision. I
was, in fact, the exception having an older child. So over the
next few years, this was our target.

To start a school we had to have some idea of the
children's problems and so that they could be taught as we
felt they should be, we had to find a teacher who held our
views on the children's basic problems. We were lucky in
that we found one early who at first taught the children in
her own little school, learning from them as she did so. We
also had to raise enough money to buy a house and to
convert it into a school and then we had to persuade local
authorities to pay fees and to provide transport for the
children. These aims were, in fact, achieved in just over
three years from the foundation of the Society, when the
teacher from her own little school moved, with the autistic
children in her care, to become our first headmistress at the
premises the Society had bought. Since then the Society has
opened many schools, local Societies have organised
themselves and have also provided schools, but as in all
things, the first step is always the most important and the
hardest to achieve.

We were fortunate that as soon as we had bought one
property, the house next door came on to the market. We
had bought the first house with money we were given by
Trusts but we had no money to buy the second house, yet it
seemed important that we should. For one thing it was an
opportunity that might not come again and for another it
would mean that we could use it as a boarding house,
immediately widening our scope because we should be able

to take very many more children. We had worked out that running a school for under twelve children would not allow us to break even and although we intended to keep the school fairly small, we should, with another building, be able to take up to twenty four. It would be more convenient, too, to use one building as a school and the other as a boarding department. So though we had no money, we bought the second house on a mortgage. It was a serious commitment for a small Society but a step which we were never to regret.

From the beginning we decided that a weekly boarding school would be more economical to run than a fully residential one. The children would come on Monday mornings and return home Friday afternoons, they would take most of their washing home with them which would be a saving— but by far the biggest economy would be in the house staff. We should need only half the number. Those who lived near enough would attend daily but, because we were accepting weekly boarders we could take children from quite a wide area. Also we would be able to help those who lived near but who, because of family problems, needed to live away from home part of the time. The small private school which David went to, with its nine autistic children, moved en bloc with the headmistress into the new Society school in September 1965.

CHAPTER TWELVE

Interests

David stayed at the Society school until he was eighteen and
for the next few years, although there were ups and downs,
life was comparatively tranquil. Paul was now independent
of course and David was fetched and returned daily by taxi
so I had more time on my hands than I had ever had.
David's headmistress was enthusiastic about his abilities
and understanding of his behaviour and Paul, after a year or
so, at last began to make progress and moved up a stream.

David was now doing ratio, square roots, percentages and
proportion in arithmetic. He and I had parted company a
long time ago and I could only provide him with straightforward arithmetic which he could check back himself to see
if his answer was correct. To amuse him I would give him
long division sums that would take the whole of a foolscap
page to solve. He would still not read for pleasure although
his reading ability was normal. He really did not understand
very much but was fond of comics. The pictures helped to
explain the text of course and this was the attraction. At least
comics gave him a normal activity which he could enjoy and
autistic children have very few normal activities.

It was now that David, who up to this time loved classical
music, began to develop an interest in 'pop'. Did he know
that this was the normal thing for his age and wish to be like
others? Meanwhile Paul had become interested in classical
music so did David feel, perhaps, that this was Paul's
province and not his? Whatever the reason, David's interest
in pop lasted until he was twenty one and then he reverted to
classical music once more, though he still listens to the 'Top
Twenty' or 'Top Forty' on Sunday evenings.

One day when he was about thirteen and was with me
while I was cooking, he suddenly said 'B'. I couldn't think

what he meant at first and then it occurred to me that he
might mean the noise the fork was making against the bowl,
so I tried other noises and sure enough, he told me what each
one was. We do not own a piano, so we had no means of
checking whether he was right or not but as soon as we did
get the opportunity we tested him, to find as we expected,
that he was quite correct. If we struck A sharp he would tell
us that it was between A and B. He didn't mind which octave
we used. Later he was able to say in which key a piece of
music was being played.

The argument as to whether David was autistic or aphasic
had been resolved some time previously. Now it was
accepted by most psychiatrists and other workers in this
field that autistic children have a severe handicap in
communication, that in fact, autistic children like aphasic
children, have great difficulty in the comprehension and use
of language. Autistic children show far wider communication problems, however, and it was now clear that David
showed the classic autistic pattern. When David was young,
of course, it was thought that autistic children really could
understand language, that they were suffering from
emotional deprivation and not an organic handicap.

With both boys these years ran one into the other so that it
is diffficult now to recall the sequence of events, though it is
easy to remember various incidents, major and minor. I was
told on Open Days that Paul was anti-social as he did not
want to join in any of the after school clubs or sports. The
school had a number of activities of this kind but Paul had no
wish to engage in them. Later, as his interest grew, he went
to orchestral concerts with parties from his school and also
joined a music club.

The headmistress had found that David was clever with
his hands and arranged for him to go to a nearby technical
school for woodwork lessons. These he enjoyed very much.
The master was pleased with him and many of the things he
made were useful, in fact I still have some of them today. I
have no doubt that the master had to stand over him to
achieve these results and I'm sure that the other children

thought him strange. He could only manage a normal environment for short periods and with help.

When the school moved to its new home David had to leave and it was necessary to wait six months or so until new contacts could be established. Again, luck with the help of the headmistress came to our aid. She found a school with a most understanding metalwork master who was willing to teach David once a week. This school, though in the same borough as his special school, was some distance away and it was arranged that I should drive him there early every Thursday morning and take him back to his school after his lesson. The metalwork master was fascinated by David and soon learned to understand him. He found that he was capable of fine and intricate work but that he needed constant supervision; a one-to-one relationship again. If left, he was unable to carry on to the next stage of work.

While David was having his lesson I would go shopping, or more usually window shopping and have a cup of coffee. It was on one of these mornings that I bought a bath rack and was told by David more than a year later than I had bought it on 19th May 1966. It was then that I realised that he seemed to know the dates on which even the most insignificant events took place. It was at this time, too, that he began to ask people the date and year of their birth and then tell them the day of the week on which they'd been born. He had been studying calendars for some time and I think that he must have learned some key years. It was obvious that some working out was necessary. He would take a little while and mutter under his breath to get some dates while others he could give almost immediately. He couldn't tell me exactly how he did this and a bit of thought shows that it is no simple process when one had to allow for leap years. He can manage to match day and date for a hundred years or more—past and future. We've had to impress on him that he mustn't ask females over 21 for their year of birth!

It was just before he was fourteen that the first signs of puberty began and the change was so rapid it took us by surprise. All at once it seemed, his voice broke, he needed to shave at least occasionally and he grew out of all his clothes missing one size in shoes on his way up. He did not seem to be particularly upset by this and the emotional upsets we had been expecting, before, at and after this time did not materialise. This is not to say that he was never disturbed but as far as it was possible to tell the disturbance he showed did not appear to be connected to adolescence but rather to things which happened to him during these years. He had settled down at school and was happy.

However, he had noticed that there was another sex and this proved slightly worrying because he did not have the normal inhibitions and was attracted to little girls of about five. He would grin happily, looking enormous when he stood by them and if not stopped would pat them. This was unlikely to worry the little girls as he was so gentle but alarmed us and would have alarmed the children's parents. We had to explain to him that he was far too old for little girls of this age. He'd been told the facts of life but it was difficult to say how much he understood or how much relevance they had to the way he felt. Fortunately, he fell for a little girl at school and this, because the children were well supervised, was less worrying for us. He asked if he could make her a bracelet at his metalwork classes.

CHAPTER THIRTEEN

Leaving School

Just before David's fifteenth birthday, I started to work part time for the Society. I was lucky, because my hours were from 10 a.m. to 3.30 p.m. and I was able to have school holidays off. This meant I was always home before David and Paul arrived from school.

The following winter Paul caught pneumonia. It had started with what appeared to be an attack of his usual tonsilitis and the doctor came and confirmed this but he didn't make the usual quick recovery. We didn't like to call the doctor at the weekend and even when he came on Monday he couldn't find anything at first. It wasn't until I said that I was sure that this attack was different that he diagnosed congestion of the lungs. Paul was quite ill but the right drug had a miraculous effect and before I knew it he was sitting up in bed demanding food. His pyjamas and bedclothes were wet through every night, however, and he didn't wake me but got up and found dry things. My husband had installed central heating two years previously so I wasn't as worried by this as I might have been.

I thought that Paul's puberty would be later than David's. He was smaller and I somehow expected him to be a late developer. But I was wrong. He, too, began to develop before he was fourteen and grew even taller than David though he was of a smaller build. The house seemed full of large people and appeared to shrink in consequence. Paul too, had a quiet adolescence and the next year or so passed relatively peacefully. We went, one Sunday, up to Northamptonshire to visit my husband's relatives and when he arrived home, David complained of feeling sick. He went upstairs and I made some supper. I hoped that nothing was wrong.

David was sick all night and the doctor diagnosed gastric flu. He stayed at home for a few days and then went back to school and I forgot about it. Several weeks later, at tea time on Sunday, David went white and complained of feeling sick. He certainly looked it, so I let him get down from the table and go outside. In a short while he came back, looking well and ate a normal tea. It worried me a little for this began to happen every few weeks. It was Paul who pointed out that it only occurred at tea time on Sundays or occasionally during the night. After this, I would tell David not to be silly; that there was nothing the matter with him—and there wasn't. It was an instant cure.

It was at this time that David began studying for two CSE's. It had been hoped that he'd be able to take an 'O' level in maths, but one look at the papers was enough to show us that he wouldn't be able to understand the language the questions were couched in. Not that the language in the CSE examination was a lot easier. It was decided that he should also take Art. His drawing was rather of the Grandma Moses type but he was very neat fingered and good at craft and this would be taken into account. In the event he passed both exams, getting a grade 2 rating in each. For Art he did a lino cut in three colours which needed the utmost precision. The examiners also visited the school to look at the craft work he had done during the year. Our education officer wrote to David congratulating him. We thought this unusually thoughtful.

Just before he was eighteen the specialist felt the time had come for David to leave school, though he could have remained for a further year. The headmistress went to see the employment people. Several things were investigated, but in the end it was decided that he should go to the Industrial Rehabilitation Unit for assessment. IRU's were originally established to help people who for one reason or another had not worked for some time, or who wanted to change their jobs but had no idea what they were fitted for. More recently they have been accepting mentally handicapped and mentally ill people for assessment, the only proviso being that the person to be assessed must be able to travel to the IRU without assistance.

David did not have a happy last term at school. He dreaded leaving and would not be reassured. He began to find eating difficult, he constantly wanted to sip water and he seemed to be awake half the night and kept us awake too, by wandering around. He became extremely difficult on his journey to and from school. He complained of feeling sick and began worrying the driver and the escort to bring him straight home before dropping the other children off.

A few weeks before the end of term I took him by tube to the IRU. The journey was very long and there seemed to be no simple way of getting there. It was not made easier either by David getting into a panic and asking to get out every few stations. I began to wonder if the whole thing were feasible. The IRU seemed in a very inaccessible place. It was locked up, of course, that Saturday, but we looked around. Not far away was a bus stop and I saw, on a timetable attached to it, that there was a bus that David could catch that stopped outside a tube station on our local line. This made a world of difference.

The next few weeks were taken up with teaching him how to get there. First we went together and I showed him where to wait and which bus and tube to catch and where and how to cross roads. The next step was to enlist the help of a friend. I would see him on to the tube and then get into the car and drive to the IRU and wait at the bus stop; she would meet him off the tube and see him on to the bus. This was done in both directions. Then she would see him on to the tube and drive to the IRU and I would 'hide' outside the tube station and watch him cross the road and catch the bus. Finally, we just kept our fingers crossed and he did it on his own.

At eighteen years old David left school and, after a short holiday, began his new life. Strangely, as soon as he actually left school, his anxiety ceased and he began to eat and sleep normally once more. I was allowed to go to the IRU with him the first day as I had an appointment with the social worker there. After that he was on his own.

The hours were 8 a.m. to 4 p.m. and we had to allow over an hour for him to get there. This meant his leaving home at 6.45 a.m. David had to do this on his own. I find it almost impossible to get up very early; so he had the alarm clock, gave himself breakfast and left. After his first day there I rang the social worker and she told me that all was well. I asked if someone could see him across the road outside the IRU as it was a busy one and there was no pedestrian crossing or central refuge.

The second morning he left on his own and I checked and found that he had arrived safely. Everything seemed all right. However, that afternoon he wasn't home at 5.30 p.m. as he should have been. I rang, but of course there was no answer. There was nothing I could do but wait. At 6.45 p.m. David arrived, looking a little strained. When I asked him where he'd been he said 'Piccadilly Circus'. He was not able to tell me *why* he'd been there and the social worker couldn't make any suggestions, though she said she would try to find out. On Wednesday he arrived at the IRU safely, but once again he arrived home at 6.45 p.m. saying that he'd been to Piccadilly Circus. The next night I went to the IRU and watched him leave, he seemed to be in a hurry—in fact he ran across the road between traffic, to my alarm—though he seemed to be watching carefully. I saw him catch the bus and I returned home feeling sure that he'd be in at 5.30. p.m. But he wasn't. At 6.45 p.m. he came in saying that he'd been to Piccadilly Circus again. Fortunately this was the last time. It took a little while to find what had been happening. The first two times it seemed that not only was he being seen across the road as I had asked but he was also being helped on to the wrong bus. Nearly all the people at the IRU caught a different one from David and whoever saw him across the road assumed that he wanted that bus too. David would not have known how to explain that he didn't go that way, so presumably he went on until he saw an underground station and then got off and caught the tube, having to go right to the centre of London to make a connection with our local line. The third time, apparently, and David was able to tell me this himself, was because the bus stopped short of the place on its destination board and once more, he found a tube station and came home by train. After that there were no further problems. Fortunately I had sewn a 50 pence piece into his coat lining for emergencies and replaced it each time it was used, so that he had enough money for the extra fares. He stayed at the IRU for six weeks and at the end of that time we were told that they considered he would do best at a Remploy workshop. We too were happy, as we felt that this would suit him very well.

Remploys are sheltered workshops which were set up after the war for disabled ex-servicemen. Now they take people who for one reason or another, cannot quite manage normal employment, though they are expected to do almost a normal day's work. In other words they are to some extent sheltered but only marginally so and the employees get normal rates of pay. His name was put down on the waiting list for the local Remploy and again I taught him, with help, how to reach it. In the meantime he travelled to a local occupation centre for three days and back to school for two days a week where he did odd jobs such as packing up boxes and cutting the hedge. He learned to travel to these places on his own. He now coped very well with tubes and buses and only needed showing once or twice. He travelled in the evenings to night school to attend art and woodwork classes and to a youth club. Every Saturday afternoon he went shopping, usually to the local record shop. After a while as we hadn't heard from Remploy, we decided that he'd be better off at the local Adult Training Centre, a sheltered workshop for the mentally handicapped. Although transport was laid on we decided that as he enjoyed his independence, he should be allowed to get there and back under his own steam.

About a year after David had started going to the training centre I found that he wasn't getting there until lunch time. It was true that he didn't leave home until 9.15 a.m., so that he didn't have to cross the busy road during the rush hour and that he had to change buses half way, but even so he should have been there by ten at the latest. He would arrive, too, without any money. The supervisor at the training centre found that he was being met by a local trouble maker and led around the town. His money which included cash to pay for his lunch and his return fare was being taken from him. On investigation I found that his diary told the whole sad story. David was quite able to deal with a situation of this sort. From that time on he had to travel on the transport provided.

As a parent of a handicapped child one sees human nature in the raw. Because autism is not yet fully understood and because all mental handicaps are suspect by lay people, parents of autistic children are particularly vulnerable. Before I mention the exceptions I must say that though one meets unkindness one also has the opportunity for seeing people at their best. One is very dependent on others and nearly everyone we met was considerate, some people doing far more than they needed to help us. To them, all one can say is a heartfelt thank you and hope that if we are never able to repay them, we will pay back the debt by helping some other parent who is desperate.

One also meets people who don't intend to be unkind but who have no idea how you feel and are therefore thoughtless. They ignore the child or will talk of him as if he is some sort of subspecies who is not worth noticing or helping. But by far the worst sort of offender, fortunately only rarely met, is the person who is malicious, who understands how you feel only too well and yet seeks to hurt by getting at you through your child.

However, parents do learn to grow pretty tough skins through sheer self defence and most of the time they are not seriously affected by the behaviour of others. It is when the child is young and they are still learning to cope that they can be badly hurt.

It was when David was twenty one that we decided to leave London. Paul was almost twenty and had to stay because of his work. We would have preferred not to have left him on his own for another year but we found him a room locally and hoped for the best. We had bought a plot of land in the same village as our cottage a couple of years previously and my husband intended to build a house. Meanwhile we were to live at the cottage and I would be able to continue with at least part of my work from there.

The move took place on a sunny day early in summer. David settled down happily and we did not foresee any problems. We visited the local Training Centre and were informed that as soon as there was a vacancy we would be notified. After we had been at the cottage a month, David asked when we were going back to our suburb of London. He had, of course, been told that we were leaving for good and he'd appeared to understand this. After six weeks he began to panic, showing almost the same symptoms as he had shown when it was time for him to leave school. He had to eat in the kitchen, as he needed to open the back door to take deep breaths of fresh air and he wanted to sip water between each mouthful. He slept poorly and kept us awake too. He would not leave the cottage and had to undo the top button of his shirt and loosen his tie. Gradually these symptoms diminished but when he was at his worst we had word that there was a place at the Training Centre, which of course we had to turn down.

One of the more worrying characteristics of David's handicap has been the length of time that it takes him to work through a fear or a habit. He seems more severely affected than most in this respect. These particular symptoms remained for a year and then lessened very gradually. Even now, several years later, they have not entirely gone and many never do so completely.

This has not meant that he is difficult to cope with. He is a great help to us. Because of the economic cutbacks the planned enlargement of the training centre has not taken place and it is unlikely to do so in the foreseeable future though the council have made alternative arrangements which work well. David now goes at our request (he could go every day) to the ATC twice a week. On the other days he helps with the housework; in fact he does all the heavy work for me and also helps his father by mixing cement, painting window frames, shaping stone and fetching and carrying. He uses and looks after our motor mower, does the heavy digging and the painting indoors. His days are filled for him as he has very little idea of what to do with his time. If left to his own devices, he will 'play' with his tins. He has a large store of these, bent and cut into various complex shapes. He usually buys tins of polish with his pocket money and the polish is transferred to a large plastic container so that he can have the tin. Polish is a household commodity that I do not have to buy myself. His other, more orthodox hobby is music. He knows the times of all the classical music programmes and will usually take the wireless upstairs while we watch television. He has a few favourite television programmes and will suddenly appear when these are due to come on. He attends a youth club once a week and is very disappointed if for any reason he can't go. He is a good-natured boy however. Although we can see how disappointed he is, he makes no fuss. Because of this we make every effort to see that he does not miss it very often.

Now and again he stays at the local hostel for the mentally handicapped and has frequently gone to the short-stay home. His name is also down for attendance at a planned sheltered workshop (a Remploy type scheme). However, we do not know how he will take to any of these changes. Experience has taught us that he can stay a week at a hostel without problems. But experience has also taught us that this does not mean that he will accept the hostel as his home on a permanent basis without a fairly long period of anxiety which will disturb his behaviour and which will probably not be understood or allowed for.

Paul comes down to stay three or four times a year and I see him on my frequent visits to London. He is making progress at work and enjoys his weekends youth hostelling and taking part in club activities. He has helped to raise quite a lot of money for the Society. At present we have no problems but like all parents of handicapped children, especially as we get older, it is the future to which our thoughts turn. We cannot expect to go on like this for ever and to whom do we entrust David for the remainder of his life? Any attempt to move him will bring on the same symptoms that previous changes have brought. Will they be understood? Has anyone the time and patience to make the necessary allowances that have to be made until he gets over the worst or will it seem easier to put him into hospital? David does not really need this kind of care.

Having an autistic child may not be an impossible problem during one's life time but the future, especially in these uncertain days, is a very real worry.

Part II

Introduction

I have tried to give as accurate an account as possible of the way that having a handicapped child affected the life of one family. It is difficult to write without sounding as if one thinks that one has all the answers. This is, of course, quite untrue. We did what we felt was right but there are many things that I look back on with regret.

I have written this account for several reasons one of which has been to amuse myself through long quiet winter evenings. Autistic children are difficult and different, the nature of their handicap is elusive and for this reason they arouse interest. No one as yet has come up with an entirely convincing reason for the handicap. It seems that no one is sure of the underlying pathology which has caused it. We have been lucky in many ways. Most 'autistic families' have had far worse problems than those which we have had to face.

In the early days of the Society I thought that all autistic children were like David and that those things which had been shown to help him would also help other children. I found that this was just not so. While autistic children have a severe problem with communication in all forms yet they remain very different and what works with one does not necessarily work with another. However, this does not mean that it is impossible to find a method of teaching that will help the majority, though it will need to be flexible. As all autistic children need a structured environment and individual attention for part of the time then it is possible to devise a teaching programme to stretch the abilities and help lessen the disabilities of each child.

The realisation that autistic children are so very different both in the degree of handicap,[62] in character and in temperament has made me very wary of pushing my own pet theories on to other people. The decision made by each family must be respected. Some parents feel guilty if they cannot cope or do not want their autistic child at home during the holidays. If they decide that the best place is the local hospital, or if they prefer a residential school to a day school, then this is their decision. They know better than anyone just how much strain they can take and are prepared to cope with. If parents ask for your opinion then this is another matter. You can say what you feel would be best but they are not obliged to follow your advice nor must you expect them to.

Knowing what I know now it would, in some ways, seem an advantage to be able to start all over again but I'm not so sure that it would make a great deal of difference to the outcome. It does not appear that parents and teachers are able to influence the child as much as is sometimes thought.[45, 49, 51, 52] This is not to say that they have no role to play and that they should not rejoice at each new achievement. They have created the background of security which has helped to make these achievements possible and by being in the right place at the right time they will have been able to demonstrate some point to the child which proves to be an invaluable step in the learning process. They will have a greater role to play in educating and bringing up a handicapped child as he will rely on them for help. Normal children are open to many influences but autistic children are especially dependent on those with whom they are in close contact.

It is known that a structured environment, a high staffing ratio and a sympathetic atmosphere are major aids to progress both academic and social.[45, 53] However, autistic children with good potential as well as some who are more handicapped have done well in schools not geared to their needs. The way each child reacts to his handicaps, his innate intelligence, his degree of language development, temperament, social abilities and, of course, the people he meets will in the end determine the kind of person he becomes. And a severely handicapped child will still be severely handicapped, though he receives the best of teaching and has the most favourable of environments. He will no doubt benefit from this to some extent, but basically the severity of his handicap will remain.[45, 49, 51, 52]

My views have changed slightly over the years as I have watched the children I know develop into adults. New research has also modified them and will no doubt continue to do so. Yet for all this they remain basically the same and are generally acceptable to the majority of workers in the field in this country at the present time. However there are books readily available, notably by Bruno Bettetheim and Gerald O'Gorman where contrary views are expressed.

In the followng pages there are chapters on various aspects of autism and on dyslexia. At the end of the book there is a reading and reference list for those who are interested enough to wish to know more. The National Society for Autistic Children will also be pleased to advise on current literature.

CHAPTER ONE

Dyslexia

There is still in medical, psychological and teaching circles disagreement as to whether there is such a thing as dyslexia. Like autism it is often thought of as a 'middle class complaint' invented by parents who cannot face the fact that their child is not making the academic progress they expect him to make.

Dyslexia or specific reading delay, which may be a better though more unwieldly term, indicates a problem with reading, writing and spelling. Now this is not an uncommon problem and may have a number of reasons; subnormality, lack of books in the home, frequent changes of school, broken marriages, overlarge classes, psychiatric or emotional disorders, poor sight or hearing. But because all these can lead a child to have a problem with reading, does not mean that there is not a specific syndrome which causes an otherwise bright child to have a very special difficulty. Perhaps 'dyslexia' is a poor word to use, in the same way that 'autism' (which can mean to psychiatrists a person who is normal though withdrawn) is.[58] Whatever label is used, however, the problem remains. Those involved with the studies on the Isle of Wight came to the conclusion that there was validity in the concept that there was, in some children, a reading delay which could not be accounted for by IQ or entirely by psychosocial phenomena.[18] It appeared to be predominant in males especially in those who had had delay in the development of speech and language.

After this length of time it is irritating that this argument should still exist. Frequent contact with children with this problem, one would have thought, would have made its existence obvious. It is not an uncommon handicap. However it may be difficult to disentangle from other reading problems especially in large classes. There is also a trend these days towards considering the labelling of a child harmful as if it either offends the dignity of the child or is in no way helpful in finding means to overcome the problem. Yet if such a child is not labelled, how can a teacher who has had some success in teaching him, pass the knowledge she had gained to other teachers? She will not know that she has helped a child with a specific problem, using a method which could help other children with the same problem. And does the child suffer unduly by having been given a label? He must know that he is finding difficulty in learning to read and is it not this that is hurting his dignity, rather than any label that may be attached to him? Parents, too, will be helped by knowing that their child is dyslexic. They will be able to meet other parents and so get support. They will also gain some insight into their child's problem. (But what will be the fate of such children already reluctantly diagnosed, if the recommendations in the Warnock Report* are implemented?).

At one time it was thought that dyslexic children were all good at arithmetic and science and failed only in subjects for which fluent reading was necessary. But having a reading problem does not necessarily make one clever in other subjects, though it is true that those dyslexic children who have a potential for maths or science will be likely to concentrate on these. It is natural to show interest in subjects at which one is proficient. Certainly not all dyslexic children are good at mathematics, in fact many of them are poor and show a tendency to reverse the order of figures in the same way that they reverse letters, and have great difficulty in remembering their tables as they have problems in rote learning. They may, in fact, have more talent in English and the arts than in arithmetic and science. Their lack of reading proficiency is the barrier which stops them making the progress in the subjects they have the latent potential for.

* Department of Education and Science (1978) Special Education Needs. Report of the commission of enquiry into the education of handicapped children and young people. Cmmd 7217 HMSO London.

As in autism, not all dyslexic children show exactly the same pattern of abilities and disabilities nor do they necessarily show all the problems associated with this handicap. Their own unique personalities and potential for certain subjects will ensure that no two are affected in exactly the same way. This is just as true in dyslexic as in autistic children.

Dyslexic children are usually late in learning to speak [48] and when they do begin, they often use a jargon which frequently only their mothers can understand. They may have almost reached school age before they are speaking clearly and fluently. They have no problem in following gesture, facial expression and bodily stance. However, they may find it more difficult than most children to follow the speech of a person with an unusual (to them) accent. They have a tendency to twist the letter in words (melliry for merrily) and to reverse the word order in a sentence. They may be poor at remembering the names of some common objects. They may also muddle words such as brush and comb, and cup and saucer, though they will not muddle the actual articles. They will probably have difficulty in telling right from left. Dyslexic children drop behind almost as soon as they begin school because they have problems remembering their letters and the sound each makes. When the teacher tries to show them how to read they may appear stupid. Many dyslexic children find the 'look and say' method meaningless as they will not be able to remember the 'shape' of the word. If they are taught phonetics, though this may take some time because of the problem of remembering and then connecting sound with shape, they will at least be able to work out some of the words.

It is noticeable that when dyslexic children do begin to read they will have difficulty in scanning. They will therefore confuse words such as sawn and swan and left and felt. They may omit the short linking words and will have problems in breaking down long words, often guessing when the word has more than two syllables. They may appear to be reading normally if they know the story so if it is suspected that they have problems it would be best to check that they really *are* reading what is on the page.

When it comes to writing, it is common for the dyslexic child to 'mirror write'. That is, they often do not know on which side of the paper to start, and if they write from right to left instead of from left to right, they will reverse the letters so perfectly that it will be possible to hold the paper to the glass and read it. Strangely they seem not to be able to tell the difference. If shown which side of the paper to begin they will seldom do complete reversals though for a long time they may reverse 'b' and 'd', 'p' and 'q' and probably 's'. Some dyslexic children, like autistic children, are poorly co-ordinated, but this, though it may be associated, is not necessarily part of the handicap. A number do have untidy or cramped handwriting however.

By the time that the child is seven he will be considerably behind his peers and will be beginning to show an uncomfortable awareness of this. The way he shows it will depend on his personality, intelligence and environment but many dyslexic children will fool around distracting the other children and calling attention to themselves.[48] They will know that they are not stupid and will not understand why they cannot learn to do things that other children, often not as clever as they, find easy.

Dyslexic children are seldom good at team games, especially those which involve a moving ball, though they may be very agile climbers and good at athletics. They are often 'cross laterals'. Most people are right handed and their right eye and their right foot are dominant. Children who are dyslexic may be left handed yet their right eye and right foot may be dominant or they may be left handed, left footed but right eyed, or right handed, left footed and right eyed. Some are quite normal, that is, the right side (eye, hand, ear and foot) or the left side is dominant, but there do seem to be more 'cross laterals' in this group than one would expect by chance.

The dyslexic child often seems to have the opposite language handicap to the autistic child with the same IQ.

An autistic child may have no problems in learning his letters and when it comes to reading he may learn to do so mechanically, with no understanding at an early age. In contrast the dyslexic child will have difficulty in remembering his letters and will take a long time to make sense of the written word, though he will understand what is read to him. The autistic child is often good at spelling; mothers report that once her child has seen a word he never forgets it. In contrast, even when the dyslexic child has learned to read fluently (if he ever does) his spelling will let him down.[48] It is nearly always the residual handicap. The dyslexic child usually has a poor rote memory, the autistic child a good one. The autistic child's behaviour is bizarre because he isn't aware of social expectations, the dyslexic child's behaviour can be disturbed because he *is* aware of them.

Even when the dyslexic child had learned to read he may still find writing a problem because although he may have overcome the reversal of certain letters he may start the letter on its right side, thereby finishing up on its left. This will mean that he will find it impossible to join one letter to the next. But the most obvious and long lasting characteristic is poor spelling.[48] This can be very odd and quite unlike the usual spelling mistakes made from time to time by most people. All the same, if the child is not too severely handicapped he will in time learn most of the more common words although he will always need to have a dictionary within reach, perhaps for the rest of his life.

However, unless he is so severely affected that he never learns to read or his spelling remains so bizarre that he cannot use a dictionary, compared to autism, dyslexia is not a disabling handicap to anything like the same extent.

CHAPTER TWO

Degrees of Handicap

To the observer, autistic children seem very different from each other and indeed they are. Intelligence ranges from above average to be so low as to be untestable [13, 43, 58] but yet they will be seen to have much in common once the basic handicap—non communication—is understood.

The image the public has is confused also. Some people think that all autistic children have normal intelligence and are unloved and rejected by their parents and it is this which accounts for their withdrawn behaviour; others think that they are impossible to help and that they sit all day long banging their heads against the wall. One can understand the confusion when one reads some of the articles and books that have been written about these children over the last fifteen or twenty years.

In the early days the National Society, too, was confused. The parents who formed the Executive Committee were the parents of young children and professional opinion of the handicap was then very different from the views held today. Almost all psychiatrists believed that autism was caused by cold intellectual parents, that it was a handicap brought about by faulty upbringing. However some psychiatrists modified this view by believing that the child must have a tendency towards autism before it could develop. Parents were usually told that their child was severely handicapped but that there was no organic damage or defect. They were therefore able to hope that with the right education and help the child would eventually recover. It is true that some parents, even then, did not believe this but they were a small minority. Now the situation is completely reversed. There is a small minority who are not convinced that the handicap is organic or who prefer to keep an open mind. Reading the very early literature of the Society (which was founded in 1962) the former attitude is evident, reading it now shows how far these ideas have changed. It is interesting too, that there are almost four autistic boys to every one autistic girl.[34] This would seem to indicate an organic dysfunction. All young autistic children behave in a very similar way. This further confused the picture because some were known to improve enough to live reasonably normal lives. It was assumed, therefore, that all autistic children were capable of the same improvement. There was a tendency among professionals towards believing that the child would be better loved and understood if he were removed from his family and in some cases it was suggested that the child— and even the parents—would benefit from a course of psychoanalysis.

In 1966 the results of a survey in the then County of Middlesex was published. This gave an overall prevalence of 4.5 per 10,000 children between the ages of 5 and fifteen. About half the children were considered to be suffering from nuclear autism—that is, lack of responsiveness to people and an insistence on the preservation of sameness. The other children showed one or other of these symptoms but not both. It was found then and in many studies since, that a higher proportion of the parents of autistic children than one would expect by chance come from the professional or managerial classes[8, 47, 51] and this has not yet been satisfactorily explained. It has been postulated that many of the fathers are unusually single minded and therefore successful in their careers and this singlemindedness may be an autistic trait. Studies carried out on the families have not shown any particular child rearing habits[8, 11, 52] which would account for the child's condition and it seems in any case that most of the children are handicapped from birth, or become handicapped after a severe illness in early childhood.

However, the main source of confusion is the belief that autistic children are all handicapped to a similar degree. It is true that two thirds of the children are mentally retarded, but of the remaining third, half gain regular paid employment and the rest make a fair social adjustment.[52] Although half remain without speech, half learn to speak though many of these show a language disability.[52] Some reach high educational levels, perhaps going to college or university. The ratio of girls to boys has already been noted but there are even fewer girls in the less handicapped group.[3] The other variables, apart from IQ, are the character and temperament and differing abilities of the children. This should be apparent, though often overlooked. A handicap is, of course, superimposed, so that every child will react differently even if the degree of handicap is the same. Moreover, even autistic children with the same IQ will not have abilities and disabilities in precisely the same areas.

The family environment and type of education will all have their part to play in the final outcome. Without imputing that parents or teachers are to blame for the handicap it can be exacerbated or relieved, just as the tendencies or characteristics of normal children can be, by the way the family and the school behave towards the child. These influences, however, though they may modify are unlikely to change or 'cure' the child.

Autism, too, has many facets, some autistic children are more socially aware and gregarious than others.[27] They many enjoy company even though they are unable to communicate very well. Some will be placid, happy or unhappy by nature, others will be anxious or shy. Some will have good manipulative ability, others will be poorly co-ordinated, some will have good cognitive ability and most will have excellent long term memories.[58, 62] Some are more advanced academically but may score the same IQ as others, who score better on other subtests.[25]

This is why IQ tests should be used to show the areas in which the child functions well and even more important, the areas where he doesn't. Autism covers a wide spectrum of intelligence and abilities and yet in spite of this and the differences of temperament, autism is a recognisable handicap. Whether its cause is different when it is found in mild handicap from when it is found in severe is a matter for debate.[4] What is evident is that all autistic children have the same basic problem. They appear to have to *learn* to communicate in a way that no other living creature does.

CHAPTER THREE

Non-communication—Two Theories

A layman who has an interest in autism and has had the opportunity to meet many of the best known specialists in the field, has read many papers on autism, watched one autistic child grow up, met many others and has spoken to parents and teachers, will have had time to think about autism and to form some opinions.

Now a specialist interested in autism is in a difficult position when it comes to writing on this subject. He can move only slowly one step at a time, from proven fact to fact which is likely to be supported by others in the field or ones allied to it. He can make one tentative step forward to ground which he hopes will be found to be solid when thoroughly researched thus, in turn, allowing a further step to be taken. However, a layman has no such inhibitions and can jump in with both feet and sink, with no loss of reputation.

The two theories advanced—though perhaps not really two but one and a half as they seem connected—may be rubbish, but they may hold a grain of truth. Readers not interested in theories, however, will perhaps prefer to go on to the next chapter which is factual.

Is speech in man a separate function from the vocalisations made by all higher animals[5] or, over the centuries, have not the sounds made by early man developed into language as we know it today? This ability to communicate in a more complex way would be of particular use to man who is not so well adapted

as many other animals for self defence and who would
need to rely on superior brain power and to seek the
co-operation of others for his very existence. Those
who could best express themselves would be more
likely to survive, thus reinforcing the development of
the speech centres of the brain. Perhaps in a similar
way, man evolved the ability to comprehend and use
written signs and symbols.

Recent research in Canada has apparently shown
that men's and women's brains differ[35]—that
women's brains are more generalised in function and
men's more specialised. It is suggested that this is the
reason men are more severely disabled by strokes. It is
only very recently, because of smaller families, the
advance of technology (which has reduced much of
the drudgery of housework), and the difference in the
climate of opinion, that it is acceptable for a woman to
pursue a career of her own. Even so, it will almost
inevitably be her responsibility to see also to the
hundred and one minor details of running a house,
though her husband may help with the washing-up
and cooking. From the dawn of history it seems that
man has been the provider, and, because of biological
necessity, the woman the general worker, expected to
be knowledgeable in the many areas of running a
household which will include cleaning, cooking, nurs-
ing the sick, bringing up children, caring for the old,
making the clothes, and, depending on the culture,
marketing or tending the livestock or garden. In these
days, too, it is usually she, whether she has a career or
not, who remembers birthdays, decides what to have
for meals, attends to the Christmas arrangements,
holiday bookings, restocking the larder, children's
dental appointments, shoe fittings and clothes,
packing for going away (and unpacking on return),
remembering to stop the milk and newspapers—all
small things but ones which take time and energy and
ones that must be attended to. Man, in his role of

provider has been free to specialise—first in hunting for food and later in pursuing his career. He has been able to help his wife if he chooses but it is not expected nor is it demanded of him. Will not this, over the ages, have had some effect on the structures of the brain? And now that women are able more easily to follow their careers—and, supposing this pattern continues or grows over the centuries and men gradually find that pressures are exerted to get a more equal distribution of labour within the family—will the brains of men and women (assuming that they are indeed different) become more alike?

Although with the advent of 'women's lib' there have been strong attempts to prove that men and women are basically the same and it is their upbringing which has forced the difference in roles and attributes upon them, yet this seems unlikely. Women appear to have an intuitive understanding of the motives and feelings of others not often found in men, who may be more highly developed in the technical and visuo-spatial skills necessary for more specialised work. In many ways men seem simpler and more straightforward than women and appear more theoretically interested in ideals and principles than in the indivuals whose lives may be affected by these very ideals and principles. Few women, even when they have a specific and narrow ability demanding hours of concentration, would have time to pursue it for they have no 'wife' to attend to all the other aspects of life for them. Unmarried women and widows are expected to care for themselves to a much greater extent than bachelors or widowers, who often live in boarding houses or rooms where a landlady will see to the more mundane aspects of life for them. The sexes are therefore complementary over the centuries, with women taking what is generally thought to be the 'inferior' role.

But does this apparently basic difference in brain

structure account for the curious sex discrepancy in autism?
And there is a very real discrepancy. Far fewer girls are
autistic—the ratio is something like one girl to every four
boys (and in the less handicapped it appears to be more like
one to nine). There seems, too, to be an almost indefinable
difference in the form that the handicap takes. It may be that
because girls seem to be more socially aware and to have
more generalised abilities,[23] then speech, to them, may be a
more necessary tool.

Those girls who are autistic are more likely to be
severely handicapped and disturbed than boys. Is this
because that in girls, speech appears to be a more
global function? If so, then maybe they are more likely
to be upset by its non-acquisition. Moreover, if they
are less likely to specialise, they will not show the
'islets of intelligence' to such a marked degree as boys
and this will not only make them seem more
handicapped, but they will have fewer outlets with
which they can amuse themselves. However, if they
are mildly handicapped they may have enough language and innate social awareness to give them the
motivation to become normal. Boys may be satisfied
with their academic achievements and may never
have the social awareness or insight to see that their
behaviour is eccentric or odd.

But surely the ability to acquire language is an
extension of the communicative skills of higher
animals.[5] When people talk of animal behaviour
they do not separate communicative skills from social
skills—they are seen as part and parcel of the same
thing, because animal's communicative skills are
primitive. In man, language is talked of as quite a
separate function. We talk of autistic children
developing social skills and language skills and
question whether their social behaviour is delayed or
bizarre because of their lack of language or whether
their language is delayed because of their poor social
behaviour. But surely language *is* social behaviour.[21]

Where does social behaviour stop and language begin? A smile of welcome is surely the same as the word of welcome, though the word is a step further along nature's developmental scale than the smile.

What is considered to be social behaviour? Social behaviour surely, is the ability to live with others of the same species, to fit in and conform to the mores into which the person is born. Each species of higher animal has the potential for learning and it appears to be the infant who has the instinctive knowledge.[20] He will need it for his very survival. A dog or cat would not be able to force an unresponsive offspring to suckle, nor would a duck be able to teach her duckling to 'imprint'. Creatures without these instincts would not survive. A well known conservationist* recently described the behaviour of an ape born in captivity. The mother, though apparently delighted with her new offspring, had no idea what to do with him, although the baby made frantic efforts to suckle. This instinct, it seems, lies entirely with the new born—without it he would die. It is only humans who can keep their unresponsive young alive.

Humans as well as animals, are surely born with instincts, and though it seems that little is known about how, with inborn knowledge, this works, it is possible to postulate that whatever this is and whatever part of the brain is responsible for this, it is this that does not function or functions poorly in autistic children. Autistic children and adults, it has been observed, have to learn in a way no other sentient creature does, to interpret intellectually rather than instinctively not only language but the gestures, facial expressions and bodily stance of others. But this is not all—they have to learn every aspect of behaviour. They are not aware of others and may enter a room full of people as if it were empty, to fetch what they came in for, not seeming to realise that they should acknowledge the presence of others.

Almost all autistic children show a lack of eye to eye gaze

* Gerald Durrell in a late night TV talk with Michael Parkinson.

at some stage of their development. A normal child watches his mother's face to pick up clues as to the way she is feeling and to note her reaction to what he is doing. Until one can read and interpret expression what is the use of watching another's face? When an autistic child begins to realise that faces express meaning, then he begins to look at them. A normal year old infant will point things out to his mother in the full expectation that she will respond.[40] No autistic child behaves in this way though he may become absorbed in watching the shadows the leaves cast on his pram or in the sound he can make by scratching the pram cover with his finger nail.

People, too, express themselves by the clothes they wear. This is even more apparent these days now that men especially, are not expected to be so conformist. They can decide on hair length and style of dress and they can choose a fashion which expresses their personality and even the way that they feel about the world—note the long hair and beards and patched and faded jeans worn by some young men and the shorter hair and more formal clothes worn by others; a good idea of attitudes can be read from this. Less handicapped young people (as the more severely handicapped will have these decisions made for them) seem to dress entirely from habit if left to their own devices. Not only will they do so inappropriately, they will manage to look odd even if presented with the right things, perhaps doing up every button when wearing casual clothes.

It seems that normal people have a very good idea of how they look to others and what others will think of them if they behave in an unusual manner. They can stand outside themselves to some extent and monitor their own behaviour.[20, 38] Autistic people seem unable to do this as they do not read the bodily stance, expression and gesture of others very easily; they are unaware that others are judging them from their appearance and behaviour. They may walk or stand oddly, giggle to themselves as something amuses them, not stand aside to let others pass or let shop doors shut in people's faces. In other words they appear unaware of their involvement with their own species.

They seem to lack this awareness from the moment of birth. Many do not suck properly or are reluctant feeders. They may scream and not cease when picked up, apparently not aware of human intervention and unable to recognise comfort when given it. They may be 'good' babies apparently content to be left alone but undemanding because unaware that their demands will be met.[52] The child does not run to his mother after falling over [50] as he will not recognise sympathy and the young man may not tell of his fears or worries as he seems unaware that he could gain comfort or reassurance by sharing his anxieties. There is no instinctive awareness that he can make demands of others and no instinctive understanding of the need for contact with them.

Although autistic infants seem born with no instinct for interaction yet they can be taught if they are not too severely handicapped. However, it is not possible to teach every social situation which will be met during their lifetime; how to use gesture naturally and appropriately, how to walk and stand in an acceptable way and how to use all the nuances of facial expression. With normal intelligence they may learn to some extent, but these everyday actions, so unthinkingly performed by all normal and even retarded people, remain unnatural to them. Their gestures will remain 'tacked on' rather than being an integral part of the conversation. Their facial expression will be rather wooden and unresponsive to the actions of others, though when something amuses them or they see a desired object, then their faces will light up. (It would seem that using facial expression for communication and using it to express delight at something which pleases oneself are two quite separate things).

Almost all the autistic children who learn to talk prefer to speak than to use gesture. Children who know that a nod means 'yes' and a shake of the head 'no' will yet not use these methods of communication;[40] nor will they usually point to things though they will understand when others do so. Moreover, it goes much deeper than this—these gestures are obvious, the more subtle ones—the lift of a shoulder, the raising of an eyebrow, the twitch of a lip, the cough of irritation—none of these will be used by an autistic person. It seems that these forms of communication are harder to learn, if they are not innate, than speech. Autistic children learn to speak rather as others learn a foreign language, intellectually rather than with an inborn potential. However it is possible for almost anyone to learn a foreign language, but could anyone learn intellectually, with no natural innate ability, to use the complex signs and signals of stance, facial expression and gesture whereby one person expresses to another his conscious and sometimes unconscious feelings? The less handicapped may learn to speak grammatically but their speech will not only be pedantic but will probably sound monotonous or be pitched inappropriately. They will tend to stick to the well worn sentences they first knew.[40] This surely indicates how very difficult and how very unnatural the whole business of interaction with other people is to them and shows that speech, which can be learned by the brightest, is easier to understand (it does, after all, follow rules) than the more subtle forms of gesture.

But however clever, and there are a few who are brilliant academically, life will always be a puzzle to them. How can a person be taught all the rules of behaviour? The potential for learning these rules come from within and normal people are born with the ability for interpreting them. It seems that the autistic person is not.

But there is another theory. *Language, its Origin and Relation to Thought*[19] is a book that should be read by every person interested in communication and in autistic children. Ronald Englefield died recently. He did not believe, with Naom Chomsky, that there is such a thing as 'inborn grammar' or 'deep structure'. He believed that 'in any language there is a conventional way of combining words in order to express the relations between ideas. . . . (and that) the similarities, even in unrelated languages can be explained by the common features of human physiology and the common elements in the human environment'.

Englefield probably knew nothing of autism yet by discussing, very convincingly, how he believes language began, he may show why autistic people find communication so difficult. Englefield says—and his theory is eminently possible, indeed probable—that the co-operative nature of man has made him compare his body with others. He calls this the ego-alter association and he goes on to say *'it is important for without it man will not learn to imitate'*, every man must play the part of agent and respondent in turn 'Each would need to learn to understand the signs of his fellows but the ego-alter association would tend to produce a common system within a co-operating group. *Agent and respondent would have to be able to put themselves in each other's places* for a condition for progress towards real language to develop so that the respondent would think of the signs that he, when acting as agent, would use' (and vice versa).

Englefield says that the imitation of an action requires the ego-alter association. 'If a man can copy the action of another man then he must be able to transform the visual impressions that he receives into muscular reactions. . . . *and this means that there must exist in the brain a 'transferring system'* which automatically connects the visual image of the action as seen, with the effector complex which issues in the action itself'. Englefield says that it is evident that the imitation of movement both as seen and as performed was only slowly realised in the course of man's development. However, the *knowledge of his own movements and that of others 'has become linked together in the mind. . . .* imitation does not occur without a motive, though man has remarkable imitative ability. When agent and respondent are working together co-operatively the situation is favourable for communication'.

So, is it this 'transferring system' that those with autism lack from birth? Is it this 'transferring system' which can be damaged by illness in early childhood? It is becoming obvious that the autistic child is unable to put himself in another person's place and so never realises what he looks like to other people—he does not imitate other children or copy the actions of his parents as a normal child does and he has difficulty in copying movement when asked to do so.

This became obvious when the Society opened its first school and gave the children PE lessons. *Now these are the very skills, according to Englefield, man needs to communicate with his peers.*

Englefield points out that a man may learn to perform a certain task and yet, if he has learned only enough and no more than is necessary then he will be helpless when anything unexpected or unusual happens. This may explain why even the brightest autistic person fails when it comes to social situations. His responses are learned and not fully understood. The slightest deviation from the expected response on the part of others will confuse him. He will feel safer within a situation which he has learned to understand and can control.

Although these two theories are different they yet have something in common. Perhaps Englefield's 'transferring system' is man's equivalent to animals instinctive behaviour at birth. Even if one or a mixture of both, were found to be true we should still not know *why* autism happens, though we would have a better understanding of *what* it is.

CHAPTER FOUR

Social Behaviour . . . 1

Parents of autistic children, mothers especially, have often been accused of not giving enough attention to their autistic child, thereby either causing or exacerbating the handicap. But if a child seems content to be left, then it is not surprising that his mother will be glad to be able to get on with the housework in peace, especially if he has kept her up most of the night. The child, therefore, gets less attention than a normal child when he really needs more. But the mother needs reinforcement too and it is not rewarding to amuse a child who shows little response. Some autistic babies cling to their mothers but the majority do not cuddle and show little awareness of being picked up. Others are cuddly, perhaps between four and twelve months, but then begin to stiffen. Later on they may refuse to sit on their parents' knees or will not allow their hand to be held when out. An autistic child enjoys a romp or a tickle and this can be fun for a while but there has to be more to it than this, there has to be a meeting of minds at some time, some less exhausting and more rewarding point of contact for both. A normal child will not allow his mother to get on with her work. If he feels he has been left on his own too long or wants his mother's attention for any reason, he will make certain that he gets it, just by worrying until he does.

If the autistic child is the first one and the mother knows little about babies she may feel that she is very inefficient, though she will gradually come to realise that the child is not developing as he should. It will be the child's remoteness which will be the cause of her disquiet, though she may not realise this for some time.

When he does cry, it will not be the attention seeking cry of the normal baby, for when he does get attention it is unlikely that he will stop. After a while his mother will lose confidence in her ability to handle him. For the first few weeks it is possible that he will have feeding problems the most common one seeming to be a reluctance to suck. Many mothers have reported that the baby falls asleep after the first few minutes. Some seem quite unable to suck naturally and it has been known to have to feed the baby with a fountain pen filler. A few, on the other hand, do not seem to feel the sensation of fullness which stops a normal baby from overfeeding. Most autistic babies do not hold out their arms to be picked up, they may be capable of sitting but may not pull themselves to a sitting posture, their babble is deviant or diminished,[39] and many refuse solid food, perhaps for years. Others do not know how to chew and their jaws have to be manipulated to show them the way it is done.

The autistic child may be excessively fearful or may show an amazing lack of fear. But whether he is fearful or fearless, his reactions will not be normal. He will not understand his mother's efforts to reassure and comfort him so that he will become frightened of harmless objects. He will also be unafraid of potentially dangerous things as, because he is so remote and lacking in comprehension, his mother will not be able to reason with him. He will, in his isolation, not watch nor will he be aware of others so that he will be unable to model himself on them, he will not imitate actions nor will he play imaginative games.[59] He would not understand what they were meant to represent in any case, because with his lack of communication he is isolated and unaware of what is happening around him. If he wants a drink he will hold his mother's wrist and put her hand on the tap. He does not appear to realise that he could mime his thirst and that his mother would know what he meant. He will understand only the immediate physical world, the fascination of colour, sound, taste, touch and light; the sensation of physical movement such as bouncing up and down or running backwards and forwards. In other words he does not look towards other people for stimulation, thereby learning and building inner resources. He seems unaware that he can make contact or behave like others and will ignore or withdraw from other children. However he will enjoy a romp or a tickle because, this again, like running or bouncing, is an immediate physical sensation. It is noticeable, however, that although he enjoys this, he seldom demands it. It has to be the parents who make the approach.

By the time that the children are 3½ they are often at their worst. It seems that a high proportion of autistic children sink into a trough at this age, which lasts for at least a year. By the time that most are five they may be beginning to make a little sense of the world.[41] It is difficult to say how much this is due to natural maturation or to help given by parents or teachers, who by this time, are aware of the child's isolation and are making strenuous efforts to penetrate it, though they may or may not know that the child is autistic.

Most autistic children, whatever degree of handicap they have, go through this phase and it would be very difficult for a specialist, except one who has studied autistic children for years, to say which few are going to improve sufficiently to attend a school for normal children in due course, which will be able to live at home and work in sheltered conditions and which will go into subnormality hospitals because they will be too difficult and disturbing an influence at home. It is probable that those who do make progress are more likely to begin to talk before the age of five,[43, 51] though this is not always so; the less handicapped child may be the one who shows, in spite of his aloofness, marked 'islets of intelligence'. He may be unusually skillful with educational toys and because he has no wider interests, will be far in advance of normal children of his own age with them. Some may show a remarkable absorption in letters and teach themselves to read or recognise words, long before they are aware of their meaning. They may surprise their mother by, for instance, working out how to carry the maximum number of objects by finding the flattest one and arranging the others on to it in a manner that suggests they are far from devoid of intelligence. It is this behaviour which makes parents feel that, although their child may be very strange, he is not mentally retarded in the usual sense of the words. Even severely retarded autistic children, and there are many to be found in this group, will not behave as other retarded children.[46] Their 'islets of intelligence' may not be marked, yet they may have skill at manipulation far above that of a mentally retarded child of a similar level of intelligence and their alert expression, quick movements and normal appearance will be at variance with their lack of contact with others. A mentally retarded child, a child with Down's syndrome, will have as much contact with others as his handicap allows, that is, if he is very severely handicapped, then he will not have much interaction but nor will he have other skills. He will react very like a normal child of a much younger age.[40]

A four year old autistic child has no sense of property. He will rifle through people's shopping bags, run behind shop counters, grab things from shelves or cupboards. Switches or water may fascinate him so that he will run into houses turning on taps or switching on all the lights. He will do these things with an alert and normal expression. When his mother tries to stop him he may have a tantrum and scream, perhaps for as long as an hour. It is partly this strangeness that causes so much interest in autistic children that led the specialists who first noted and were interested in the condition to unlikely theories of causation.

Though some autistic children are abnormally lethargic, most are over-active. They seldom sit still for more than a minute or so and they seem to need curiously little sleep. Their parents are exhausted and usually lonely. How do they explain their child's behaviour to others? It is at this age, too, that the child is so remote that he may not recognise his parents. It is the darkest part of the tunnel.

Though the child may become a little less isolated after 5 years old,[41] he may still be severely retarded. However, most are beginning to realise that their parents are there, they may now begin to look briefly at faces; they may begin to be aware that words have meaning and the comprehension of just a few words, especially if the child has learned to use them, can make a big difference. If the child improves, tantrums become less, making education easier, toilet habits are learned—their lack of control in this and the way many have of smearing faeces on walls is one of their less endearing habits—and the parents may find that they can take the child out in public without making themselves too conspicuous.

CHAPTER FIVE

Social Behaviour . . . 2

Even though the child may become less remote after the age of five and the family can begin to lead some semblance of a normal life, yet he remains different. Perhaps inflexibility is the best word to describe even the least handicapped children. They are sticklers for routine, not surprisingly, when one realises that the world must seem chaotic to them. They have extreme difficulty in making any sense of what they see and what they hear, so that there are few things that they can rely on. It must seem then, that these few things must be held on to at all costs. The reassurance of the same cup and plate, the same place at table, the furniture in the same position, the same route to the shops, takes on immense importance especially in the more handicapped children. They will show strong reactions to new situations, they have had difficulty after all, in learning to understand what they have and they will not wish to accept any change or new experience which they will not be able to absorb quickly or easily. Paradoxically they may enjoy a complete change in routine such as going on holiday, it is changes in their usual environment that they find so distressing.[61]

Nearly all autistic children before the age of four appear to have spent some considerable time making long lines of objects. Most, instead of playing with their toys, will line them up and when they have come to the end of their possessions they will add any odd unattached household object that they can find. This line will often stretch from one end of the house to the other and mothers have reported that some children will continue it to the bottom of the garden. Very often the children become upset when parents try to intervene either by attempting to stop them or by breaking up the line. Other children play with string and will tie the doors or all the furniture together. Some make patterns with their collections of shells, pebbles or bricks. All these activities lack imagination. This lack is especially obvious when one watches a child 'playing' with a toy car. He will usually turn it upside down and spin the wheels. An autistic child will not show normal interests in dolls or playing at tea parties.[40] These activities need imagination but how can autistic children possibly use imagination when they can have no conception of a world outside themselves? Before one can imagine a thing one has to understand what things are and to be able to do this one has to be aware of and to watch others. One cannot play at 'mothers and fathers' when one doesn't realise one has a mother and father.

Autistic children usually have normal health and are very often overactive, they keep on the go all day and often most of the night. In the early years when they have overabundant energy but no play behaviour, no interaction with others and no sense of danger, they make life very difficult for their families.

Very severely handicapped children mostly do not learn to speak, nor do they learn to understand very much so that a little social training to make life a little easier is possibly all that can be achieved. The child will need life long care, and will usually go into a hospital for the subnormal. Social training will be useful and lead to a happier life wherever the child finds himself. Self help skills can be taught to most severely handicapped children and can give them some sense of achievement and dignity.

Many autistic children injure themselves. In the few who have normal nonverbal IQ's only about a third will show this symptom and of those who do, it may not be for long and will more commonly take the form of head banging or biting the back of the hand, especially if they go through a period of acute unhappiness or frustration. In the more severely handicapped, this may be a more worrying symptom. The children may pick at scabs so that wounds will not heal, they may pull out their eyelashes or their hair or scratch at loose pieces of skin. In the very severely handicapped it may be the most worrying symptom of all as the children may be in real danger of seriously damaging themselves. The reasons for this behaviour may be different in the varying degrees of handicap. In the mildly handicapped it may be that the child is inhibited from hitting out and in his frustration will hit or bite himself. In the more handicapped it may be that even a painful sensation may be preferable to no sensation at all. Self injury usually seems to happen when the child has nothing better to do and is frequently seen when he is in an institution and unoccupied. Sometimes a child will use self injury to call attention to himself. He may find that scratching his face until it bleeds makes him the focus of attention.[9] If the behaviour is to be stopped then the reason for it has to be understood.

Most autistic children have mannerisms of some sort, but, rather like self injury, these are not so common in children with normal nonverbal IQ's. One that is frequently found in both the 'mildly' and severely handicapped is rocking and jumping up and down when excited, usually accompanied by flapping of the hands, not an uncommon sight if one watches very young children but one which looks very out of place in a ten year old. The less handicapped may grow out of these mannerisms altogether, though their movements may look wooden. Even the way they sit may not look natural and this rather stiff and awkward manner seems likely to remain throughout their lives. It is often this which makes them noticeable and may make them the butt of street gangs and bullies.[1]

Among the more severely affected and occasionally, among the less handicapped also, the fingers are flicked by the side of the face. The child will look at them from the corner of his eyes and this activity will completely absorb him. The children seem to get some stimulation from this behaviour that is difficult to replace by anything else. It is possible to stop these mannerisms while the child is occupied but it is not practical to occupy a child for every minute of the day. The behaviour contrasts oddly with the child's appearance and will call unwelcome attention to him, moreover, the bigger he grows the odder he will look. A number will walk on tip toe, especially when young. Other children are 'spinners' either of themselves or objects and become skilful at twirling the most unlikely things and many will dangle a string or carry a stick around with them. Unravelling wool and tearing paper are common habits. Some children grimace but this is apt to come and go. Others seem interested in hands, their own or other people's, and they may stare at them or sniff them. In fact most autistic children like either to touch, smell or listen to things. Rather like deaf or blind children, they use the senses that are intact. Touch seems especially important to them. They enjoy feeling smooth surfaces and often have a passion for touching fur or hair.

Some autistic children, especially when young, seem not to feel pain, heat or cold so that they must be even more carefully watched as they may inadvertently injure themselves or go outside in subzero temperatures with no clothes on. It is common for autistic children with all degrees of handicap to take their shoes and socks off and many will take their clothes off too. Others seem unduly afraid of hurting themselves which makes them unadventurous, some feel the cold so that it is difficulty to get them away from radiators. They may fear feeling cold too, so that they will refuse to wear short sleeved shirts or to take off thick woollies in a heatwave.

Rigid and obsessive speech (if the child is not mute) and rigid and obsessive behaviour will be found at all levels of handicap. Many children, mostly among those who are less affected will insist on complicated rituals,[4] perhaps before going to bed or before a meal. Others are obsessed by certain objects or topics of conversation and it will be difficult to interest them in anything else. Many, but not all, show from their earliest years, a deep love of music. If they had been normal, with all the outlets and interests a normal child has, then they might never develop this gift to any extent but it seems probable that when it is the only interest, it may become the most important thing in their lives. Children with this talent are fortunate, at least it is a normal one and one that they are able to indulge easily just by listening to radio or record player.

Most will collect objects, ones that are usually of no value whatsoever, but they will go to great lengths to get them. The kind of objects that are sought are plastic washing up liquid bottles, tin lids, holly leaves and cellophane paper— but it can be anything. The collecting and hoarding habit is a deeply ingrained one, even some autistic adults who are able to lead independent lives are loath to throw anything away so that their rooms become full of junk. They seem especially attracted to old newspapers, timetables and books but they may hang on to quite useless pieces of broken furniture. Many moderately handicapped adults living at home become adept at making little caches because they know that their parents will want to put the offending objects into the dustbin.

If one thinks as the brain as a computer, the brain of the autistic child must have very little 'input' and therefore very little data to process and to 'output'. It does seem though, that the storing and retrieval of memory is normal. Even severely handicapped autistic children seem to have good memories and some have memories that are exceptional. This shows itself in some by the way they remember the route to a place they have only been to once before and in others by humming an aria from an opera they have heard on one occasion only, by repeating conversations that they heard a month previously, by remembering lists of names and dates and by recognising people that they have not seen for several years. It may be that as the children have little meaningful 'input' to process, memory is able to take on a more important role.

Although there is little meaningful 'input' it seems that the children have difficulty in processing the data that they do have. They cannot easily 'rethink'. Once a thing has been learned or seen in one way it is difficult for them to visualise it in any other way. Some children can replace, in the exact order, what appears to the normal eye a haphazard jumble of bricks [58] and if parents disturb this arrangement they can become very upset. With many the way they see or understand a thing the first time is the 'right' way. It may be one of the reasons for the objections to any changes in their environment. It is a trait that like many, can be seen through the whole spectrum of the handicap. A moderately handicapped child will continue to use the same well worn sentences even when he has the language ability to rephrase them and a less handicapped child may become upset if any 'fact' that he has learned is proved to be wrong.

An autistic child is inflexible. This is surely the understandable outcome of being born without the instinct for interaction with others and therefore having to learn to live by rules.

CHAPTER SIX

Language Development . . . 1

Communication includes gesture, bodily stance, facial expression and spoken language; the whole gamut of human social interaction. Yet spoken language though central to, and part of, social behaviour, can be observed in isolation. However, it is difficult to separate language from other forms of social interaction in the first years of life which may support the contention that speech is only an extension of the social communication shown by all higher animals.

Autistic babies appear to be born without the potential for learning to understand or use speech just as they are unable to communicate in other ways. However, lack of speech is not obvious from birth as other forms of communication and interaction are.

But speech is what differentiates man from other animals and when the lack of understanding and use of speech is compounded by a lack of all other forms of language—gesture, expression and bodily stance [51]—it is no wonder that autistic children are isolated from their parents and from their brothers and sisters.

All autistic children have a communication problem though some learn to talk and to comprehend more easily than others. In most, however, understanding speech is a difficult obstacle, for unless one has the potential for learning it, it is not a skill that is easily acquired. Most autistic children are suspected of being deaf when they are young and it takes a little while to sort out as they are not co-operative when it comes to testing. Deaf babies may not be able to hear but the part of the brain which has the potential for developing communicative skills is usually intact and deaf children will learn to communicate with, and understand others, by visual methods. The same is true of blind babies who will soon learn to read inflection and subtleties in a person's voice. To be autistic is similar to being born both deaf and blind. But even this is not a true analogy. Autistic children do not have the inborn potential for communication that children born both deaf and blind have. Autism is a handicap apart in more ways than one. Autistic children are lone children.

Once the first few difficult weeks after birth have passed many parents of autistic children have reported, retrospectively, that their child responded almost normally for a while, though most parents did not lose their sense of unease entirely. Is it that the child can almost cope at this age and is it because life becomes too complicated as speech begins to play a larger part that the child begins to retreat around the age of 12–18 months? Is it often at this age that the child begins to look 'through' rather than 'at' the parents and it is the age when he begins to drift into the severe isolation which is usually at its worst between 3 and 4. A normal child will be able to comprehend quite a lot that is said around this age, words will be playing a far larger role than previously; he will watch his mother closely and when he is out in his pram, he will point to things and will expect a verbal response (behaviour conspicuously absent in autistic children). He will be beginning to understand and react much more to speech in his environment.

The autistic child, on the other hand, will not attempt to speak (in fact his babble will not have been normal), or he may say a few words and then stop probably because the words mean nothing to him. He may have been cuddly, but now he may stiffen when held, he is becoming more remote. Is he not making sense of words? In some way are his attempts at communication not being reinforced? No human being will persevere with an apparently meaningless activity for ever. If the child cannot understand what people are saying, then he will not be able to join his family and will remain isolated.

Most autistic children who can talk are echolalic, that is, they repeat sentences they have heard maybe as long ago as a month previously in the same accent and tone of voice used at the time. The sentences, which are sometimes quite long, may sound random though in fact they may be loosely relevant; that is, the child is perhaps reminded by circumstance, of the previous occasion and be motivated to repeat the words heard at that time. The words may have been given emphasis so, though not understood, they will have made an impression. Two examples of this are given later in this chapter.

Autistic children often show immediate echolalia. If asked 'Hullo, how are you?' they will reply 'Hullo, how are you?' Research has shown that autistic children can remember a nonsense sentence more easily than can a normal child.[28] It is obvious from this that they really do not understand the meaning of words, that they cannot break a sentence down into its separate components. A child who wants a biscuit will say 'do you want a biscuit?' because this is what people say to him when he is given one. When one stops to consider, it is amazing that the normal child does not do this also but has the ability, and an ability which appears to be lost later, to learn grammatical patterns[6, 32, 36] and to realise that words can be changed around[32] to suit the situation. Recent research has shown that babies learn to comprehend intonation[12] and are aware of language far earlier than is generally realised and normal babies will move their mouths as if trying to copy speech from two to three months old when people talk to them.[56] This innate potential for learning to talk and to understand is quite absent in autistic children. Those who learn to speak, and not all do by any means, seem to have to learn in a painstaking way rather as an adult learns a foreign language and a foreign language quite unlike his own (indeed when he does not have a language at all). Some autistic children do not suffer from echolalia to any great extent but they will show the same difficulty in learning to use and comprehend and use speech, in fact they may not have the same facility for reproducing words and may be rather silent children.

All autistic children, echolalic or not, have to learn the meaning of words and this is usually a slow process, although some show more proficiency than others. Though this proficiency is not necessarily associated with intelligence, it frequently is.[43] One of the difficulties is that autistic children do not realise that speech is important so that other sounds in the environment take on an equal significance. Moreover, if they are constantly subjected to conversation that is over their heads they will 'shut off'[46, 52] just as normal people learn to shut out adventitious noises such as machinery or traffic when they are working or listening to other people. The advice to keep on talking to the child so often given in the past—and sometimes still today—is only useful if the speech is meaningful to him.

A normal child has a terrific urge to be understood and even if he is not born, as Chomsky suggests, with 'deep language structure' he experiments by listening to others and then by twisting words and sentences until they make sense and he gets a response. He has enormous flexibility. His communication ability comes from within, whereas in autistic children it is imposed from without.

Most autistic children appear to be extremely sensitive to sound. It is noticeable, however, that this need not necessarily be loud. Some children seem more upset by a quiet continuous noise; for instance the hum made when the test card is displayed on television is one that a number of children especially the less handicapped find particularly distressing. Most of the children put their hands over their ears. though many only partially cover them, thus damping down the sound without entirely excluding it. It seems that the children do not find it easy to differentiate between noises which should be meaningful to them and those which are not. Parents have noticed, too, that the children often seem to be able to understand far better what is said to them over the telephone. Is this because the sound goes directly into the ear and they are not distracted by other noises in the environment? And why is it that some children seem to understand better when words are sung rather than said?

It is very easy for parents to think that the child

understands more than he does. This is because he picks up visual clues from his surroundings. If he sees that the table is laid for a meal, then, when he is asked to come and have lunch, he will comply. This does not mean that he has understood what was said, it is likely that he would have responded in the same way if his mother had said 'Come upstairs with me'. Two well known instances illustrate this lack of comprehension and parents can give many others. One little boy would shout whenever he was about to be scolded for some minor misdemeanor 'don't throw the dog off the balcony'.[30] He had been told, probably in a sharp voice, which made an impression, not to throw his (toy) dog. Similarly a little girl would say, whenever she was upset, 'rabbits don't cry'. This mystified the people who were caring for her until they discovered that her mother, to calm her, would point to her toy rabbit and tell her that her rabbit didn't cry. These remarks naturally surprise people, but they show clearly that the child has not understood the words but has some idea of the context in which they were used and a similar situation will trigger off the same response.

It may sound from what has been said so far that autistic children have no problem with articulation and the fault lies with comprehension only. This is not so. Many autistic children are not able to pronounce words that they do know. Not only do many have articulation problems, they also have problems with intonation. Most have very monotonous voices, not unlike deaf children's, and they speak rather too loudly. When they try to use inflection they frequently raise and lower their voices in the wrong places, except when they are echoing a sentence used by another person.

Young children often leave the ends off words. 'Juice' will become 'ju' for instance and some words will be quite unrecognisable. A few children have been helped by learning to read and will want to see a word written down before they attempt to pronounce it.

The child who is beginning to make progress with language will still have immense difficulties. He may confuse

questions such as 'How are you?' with 'How *old* are you?' A
sentence used to convey certain information or instruction
will have to stay in the same form, too, as changing 'hang up
your coat' to 'put your jacket on the peg' will be so different
that it may well have been spoken in another tongue. He
may not recognise that 'feel' and 'felt' and 'think' and
'thought' are the same verbs and will understand only
'feeled' and 'thinked'. He may be put out when he finds that
the plural of sheep is not 'sheeps'. It is evident that he tries to
make rules for language as very young normal children do
but where a young child learns quickly and corrects his
mistakes without comment as soon as he is given the right
word, it is a laborious process for the autistic child and
happens when he is much older if he ever reaches this stage
of development.

The language development of autistic children is abnormal; they have no real 'feel' for it.[57] What normal child asks
what 'and' and 'the' mean? He uses them as a matter of
course (although this may be because he will learn to use
them before his is old enough to query their meaning). But
autistic children are late talkers and many remain mute.
Very few learn to speak fluently and grammatically,
although they may be able to make themselves understood.
However the acquisition of the use and comprehension of
even a few words should not be underestimated. It can make
all the difference to his family who will, perhaps for the first
time, have some inkling of what he wants or how he feels.
They may also be able to give him simple instructions or
information and sometimes even a simple explanation can
avert an hour's tantrum.

CHAPTER SEVEN

Language Development . . . 2

How do parents and teachers cope with a child who does not understand language—that is, how do they set about teaching something that is normally learned as a matter of course? First they have to realise that the child does not comprehend what people are saying. Now this sounds like stating the obvious, but in fact it is very easy to think that the autistic child does understand what is being said and strangely, if the child is mute, it is easier to think this than if he can speak. Once he starts to talk, the very way he does so will show how poor his comprehension is. But a bright, alert non-speaking child who seems wrapped in deep thoughts of his own can easily lead teachers into thinking he 'won't' rather than 'can't'. Some teachers like some parents will be certain that the child understands all that is said and this conclusion is often based on little more than that the child will sit down when the teacher pulls out a chair for him. If parents and teachers are asked whether the young child likes hearing a story read to him, the answer will usually be no—in fact, if the child is at nursery school, story telling time will be most difficult and in all probability will be when he runs round the room distracting the others.

Having established that the child does not understand words, the first step will be to 'label' objects. Once the child realises that an object has a label which can be attached to it he may acquire a large vocabulary of nouns quite quickly. It will be sensible to teach the most common ones first, of course. There is not much point in teaching a child the names of objects that he is unlikely to see very often or not at all, or at least not until he has acquired a large vocabulary of everyday nouns. Autistic children do not generalise well, so it may be necessary when one names 'table' for instance to show him several—if possible ones with two, three or four legs—and pictures of tables, too. He can be shown the written word at the same time as some autistic children learn to read easily. Some become quite excited when they find that things have names and will run around touching objects, wanting them labelled. Because their memories are usually good, they are unlikely to forget them once they have learned them.

This sounds a big step forward but on reflection it will be seen that a list of nouns does not help greatly, though it will make some difference and will perhaps give the child a vague concept of what language is. The next logical step is to teach verbs in much the same manner, although this time parents or teachers will have to act hopping, skipping, sitting, running and walking and so on. Again, these are quickly understood, depending on the child's degree of handicap of course. A one-to-one relationship is essential when trying to teach anything at this stage and before the parent or teacher begins it will have been necessary to break into the child's isolation,[52] if needs be by crawling round the floor after him or by parent or teacher putting herself into the middle of the child's 'run' between wall and door so that he will have to notice her presence. It is usually a waste of time waiting for the child to make the initial approach, if he'd known how to he would have already made contact with her. Weeks and months can be lost in this way to no useful purpose. It is best if the parent or teacher gets her head on a level with the child's so that when he turns towards her her face will be seen and will begin to mean something to him.

The common verbs may be fairly quickly learned once demonstrated but a verb and a noun, though useful, will not really facilitate normal conversation. The autistic child does not seem to have that sense of 'sentence pattern' that Chomsky says a normal child has. He may learn nouns first and then verbs as a normal child does—except that unlike a normal child he does not 'pick them up' but has to be taught them—but he has no flexible framework to fit them into; or he hasn't the language ability or flexibility of thought to experiment or play with words. This again is another factor which leads to the rigidity autistic children show.

After verbs, adjectives appear to be the easiest, then adverbs and some prepositions. It will be apparent that all the things which can most easily be taught can be seen either by demonstration or by touching them. Colours, if the child realises that the word 'blue' means the colur and not the object itself, are usually learned quickly; adjectives and opposites such as long/short, big/little, fat/thin; adverbs such as quickly, slowly, quietly; prepositions like on/off, under/over, behind—which can be shown are learned, though perhaps with difficulty—but as soon as one comes to anything abstract then how does one teach it? How does one show 'unless' and 'until' for instance? Normal conversation is full of abstract words which is why autistic children find it so difficult. Instructions are usually concrete however and these are very much easier for the children to follow although it seems hard for them to remember more than one instruction at once. This is odd, as in other ways they have exceptionally good memories. It may perhaps have something to do with their single track minds, or by the way, perhaps, that they have been shown to have a tendency to remember only the end of a sentence.[28, 51]

Many people have remarked on the telegrammatic speech of autistic children. This is because they use only the words that are meaningful to them—that is, the concrete words. The little linking words such as—and, also, the, as, to, a, of, but, such, if, even, it, so, though, etc. will have no meaning and will be omitted. The varying tenses of verbs will not be understood so that sentences with phrases such as 'he would have had' will be far too complex for them to follow. The young child will not be able to ask 'What is this?' a very abstract collection of words. If he wants, for instance, to know what he is to have for lunch he will say 'fish?' and wait to be contradicted, running through a week's menu if necessary until he hits on or is told the right thing.

It is interesting to consider how a normal baby learns language. He has to start from nothing as he knows no language at all. He has to learn the sounds and their meaning, the subtleties of inflection, articulation, pronunciation and grammatical structure. He does all this in a few years. Later, when he is older, he will find it an intellectual exercise to learn a foreign language and he is unlikely to lose the accent of his mother country, his mouth and tongue will somehow fall into the pattern learnt early in life. Yet as an infant he may learn three different languages at the same time and not become confused. There must be some facility for language which begins to disappear in early childhood, perhaps as early as 3½ or 4 years of age. Some autistic children of normal non-verbal intelligence, may learn to speak grammatically using quite normal and complex language. They somehow make the jump between the concrete and the abstract and by their teens their speech is basically normal. However, although the sentence structure may be grammatically correct it may be almost too perfect. Somehow the inflexibility which is found in other areas is also present in language. The grammatical rules are followed so well that their speech is pedantic and formal. Innuendo or inflection is not usually understood and there are difficulties in making sense of proverbs. They remain, in spite of the acquisition of language, in a narrow world and can talk only about subjects which interest them. The less handicapped find difficulty in interpreting other people's reactions to what they are saying. They will never know when they have said too much or too little [15] as they lack the feel for 'social' language though they may love and be fascinated by words, sometimes even inventing them. Some however, have normal non-verbal intelligence and yet never make this jump. They may have enough speech to make themselves understood and may understand others on a concrete level, but yet progress no further, although many have mathematical, visuo-spatial or other skills. Why is it that some can learn abstract speech and others, with apparently the same level of intelligence, cannot? Lack of comprehension will inevitably lead to lack of 'input' which in turn will lead to lack of information so that the innate intelligence will have little to feed on and the young person is unlikely to progress as far as his potential intelligence would lead one to expect. The problems of the less handicapped autistic child are discussed more fully in Part II Chapter 11.

Pronouns are especially difficult for autistic children and there seem to be two separate problems. One is due to echolalia and the other to the way pronouns keep changing. An echolalic child will repeat the question when answering it; 'Do you want some orange juice?' will be answered by 'Do you want some orange juice?' instead of 'Yes' or 'Yes, I want some juice', so that the pronoun will of course be reversed. The child will also use phrases he has heard used by others when he wishes to make himself understood. This will mean that when his intention is to use 'I', 'you' will often be what he actually says. But the child who has little or no echolalia will still find pronouns difficult. This is not surprising when one realises how complicated they are. The same person can change from 'you' to 'I', 'me', 'mine' or be included in 'us', 'ours', 'yours' or 'we' all in the same conversation. One does indeed need language flexibility to keep up with this. A young child will often use his own name to avoid using 'me' or 'I' and will use proper names where he can. 'Mummy go' for instance. Very young normal children will do this too, of course, but for a much shorter time. 'What', 'why', 'how', 'when', 'where', and 'who' will also need practice.

Most autistic children learn to say 'no' long before they say 'yes'. It is difficult to say why. Perhaps this is because 'no' is a very definite and also *safe* word to use. 'No' is a blocking word, is much more positive and therefore has a clearer meaning. Instead of using 'yes' the child usually repeats the sentence or the end of the sentence for instance, 'Do you want a biscuit?', 'Want a biscuit'. 'Yes' is a much more 'open' word, commits one to a lot more and therefore has more meanings. But once the child does begin to use the word 'yes' he will then say it to almost everything that is suggested to him. It seems that he uses it rather like a radio operator uses 'Roger' for signifying 'received and understood' rather than for agreement.

Another oddity is the way that some autistic children appear to mis-hear what is said even though their hearing has been proved to be acute. They will sometimes repeat a sentence wrongly in a puzzled way and it will be obvious that they have not properly heard the words. Perhaps at one stage of their development they will watch people's lips and a young child will sometimes examine his parents' mouths as if trying to find where speech comes from.

Because autistic children have problems in understanding language, they are very literal. If asked the question 'What would you do if you cut yourself?' they will give the classic answer 'bleed'. Similarly if asked what their school is like they may offer to draw a ground plan. At the first school run by the Society the children were asked, in an art lesson, to paint the flowers—which they proceeded to do. Like very young normal children they will be only too truthful, perhaps telling an old man that he is 'nearly dead' or saying in a penetrating voice (autistic children usually speak rather loudly and if asked to speak quietly will change to a piercing whisper) 'man got no hair' or 'lady got crooked nose'. There is a wide variation, however, in the extent that autistic children will develop language. Very many parents will never meet the problems mentioned as their child will never reach the stage of development where these errors would become apparent, others will encounter them as their child progresses to more normal language, but a number will reach this level of development and make little further progress.

CHAPTER EIGHT

Education . . . 1 Special Schools

It is only since April 1971 that all autistic children have been entitled to education. How much difference this has made in practice is hard to tell, for many will still be attending units for the severely subnormal, just as they did in the past, although now they will be helped by a trained teacher. Since 1971 too, special units for autistic children, employing trained staff, can be attached to these erstwhile Junior Training Centres (now known as ESN (s) schools). The biggest difference however has been the development of the Social Services. Realistic fees are now obtainable for young people in Communities and Homes and because of this many new ones are opening although local authority cutbacks over the last few years threaten this movement.

Because autism covers the whole spectrum of intelligence, autistic children are to be found in every kind of school. However, the majority are retarded, most will need special education and even those few with normal non-verbal intelligence will benefit from special help and understanding.

Autism is not one of the special categories listed in the 1944 Education Act as being in need of special education and before 1971 the children were required to take an intelligence test at the age of five to ensure that they would benefit from teaching rather than training. Many parents had letters from their education authorities telling them that their child had been found 'ineducable' and would not be able or permitted to attend school. Some of these letters were kindly worded, most were not and parents found them distressing. This, of course, did not apply only to parents of austistic children.

Children are no longer 'sorted' and the Training Centres

are now special schools for the severely subnormal and are, these days, administered by the education authority and not the health department as formerly. The teachers have to be qualified and are trained to teach those who are mentally handicapped. All this helps. There is not the worry there once was, not quite the same fear that the child will be found 'ineducable' and that he will never get a proper chance, that he will be 'trapped' by the health department and never allowed 'education' even if he shows unexpected improvement academically. In theory this was allowed for, but in practice it was difficult to get a child reclassified as 'educable' once he had been found 'unsuitable for education in school'.

Schools for the severely subnormal have a comparatively low staffing ratio and autistic children who are non-communicating and frequently overactive do not usually fit in very well with the other children. Because their overactivity is disturbing to the others, they are often placed in special care units. These are usually found close by, indeed are often attached to the special school. Special care units take the very severely multiply handicapped children who are nearly always frail and physically disabled, so that although the staffing ratio may be a little better, a robust overactive autistic child can be a very disruptive element.

Some autistic children are judged able to attend the local school for the Educationally Subnormal (ESN (m) school). These schools take children who, it is thought, will benefit from education, but education at a slower pace than would be found in a school for normal children. Again it is the staff/pupil ratio and the child's difficulty with communication which makes these schools less than ideal in most cases.

A few autistic children go to primary schools for normal children. Some have to leave after a short while as they are just not able to cope but others manage and even transfer to secondary school at the appropriate age. Again very few are capable of this because of the staff/pupil ratio and their lack of communicative skills. Some enter secondary school after a slow start at a special school. These, and the ones who have always managed within the normal school system, are the children who make the 'breakthrough' and may be able to live at least semi-independent lives.

The time will come when some autistic children receiving special education will be thought to have developed sufficiently to move to a normal or at least to a less sheltered environment. This, of course, is an important moment and one that his teachers have been aiming for. It has also proved practical providing care is taken during the changeover.[26] The teachers at the school he is to leave will have to prepare him to make the change—and most importantly, the school he is to go to will have to be made aware of his special problems and his likely reactions to a different environment. A child who seems almost normal in a special school may not appear this way in the rough and tumble of the outside world.

Education authorities have an obligation to give special education to children suffering from a number of handicaps and for this purpose many kinds of schools have been set up. As autism is not one of the categories listed, (in fact, when the list was first devised in 1944, autism was not generally recognised), autistic children were accepted for education under 'maladjustment' and were sometimes sent to schools for maladjusted children as now and again local authorities took the label rather too literally. This was usually the worst choice of all. But autistic children are to be found in nearly every kind of school; schools for normal children and for educationally subnormal children both severe and moderate, the physically handicapped the delicate and even schools for the deaf. However it is unfortunately true, that, although there have been many exceptions, on the whole autistic children do not mix happily with normal children or children with other handicaps. It was this, and the mistaken belief that *all* autistic children had more potential than most are now known to have which made the Society decide to make its first priority the provision of schools so that the children could fulfil their potential by getting the concentrated attention that it was felt that they needed. And although it is now accepted that the majority of autistic children are retarded, many of them severely so, yet they do not mix easily with others and the need for special and 'apart' education is still valid. The findings of the comparative study conducted into the educational treatment of autistic children and published in 1973 showed that the children benefit from special .education.[45] They benefit particularly from a structured environment [45, 53, 60] and from an educational programme designed to take account of their handicaps. They benefit both academically and socially. Progress is closely related to IQ but even the severely handicapped benefit. In fact they gain more from the structure and organisation of a special school for autistic children than the less handicapped, though they will probably not learn to read or to do arithmetic.

Now several years have passed. Many parents, too young to remember the early struggle for special education for autistic children, are suggesting that their child should not be separated from other handicapped children and should be taught in schools taking children with mixed handicaps. Parents feel that other children, such as those suffering from Down's syndrome, are outgoing and happy and would have a good influence on autistic children who are withdrawn and solitary. It has not been proved that autistic children benefit from mixed teaching (in fact the findings of the comparative study perhaps suggests the opposite though this aspect was not specifically investigated [45]) but some parents feel happier seeing them in the company of other, more sociable children. Certainly there seems to be a case for letting autistic children take advantage of all social facilities for the mentally handicapped when they have developed sufficiently to be aware of and to enjoy these outings and meetings. There are normally a number of voluntary helpers present who will do their best to see that all the children are involved and indeed may ask another handicapped child, usually a less affected and more outgoing one, to amuse and look after the autistic child. This is to everyone's advantage. But does the same attitude extend to school hours' It may do in some cases, and, if this is so, then the child will be well placed and there will be no need for concern. Usually however the school will have one teacher and classroom helper to 15–20 children and even one overactive and disruptive child can be a problem. The autistic child who is quiet and withdrawn will not be so disturbing an influence but it is unlikely, considering the other pressures on the teacher, that she will have time to give him attention and unlike the other children he will not demand it. However, it is impossible to be dogmatic. Everything depends on the attitude of the school, especially that of the principal and the teacher most concerned with his day to day care.

Most autistic children have no inner resources and cannot be left to amuse themselves. For this reason they benefit from and enjoy a structured environment.[45, 53, 60] Educationalists are fond of seeing children play with sand and water, and certainly young, normal children may benefit greatly from the castles and harbours they can create from these mediums. Autistic children seldom do anything with sand except run it through their fingers or throw it round the room, although they may enjoy filling and emptying containers with water. However, they do not play imaginatively[40]—they are unable to—and it is very doubtful if sand and water play does anything for them.

A great deal of thought has to be given to the teaching materials used. Very often teachers will have to devise or adapt the equipment they need for teaching. They will have to work out how to keep each child occupied, for they will lapse into their obsessions if given nothing to do. Although there will be time for free play each day, it will be noticeable that the children do not play together unless someone is there to organise them and though the playground may have twenty children in it, each will be absorbed in his own little world.

Yet for all this, they are aware of each other and will notice if one of their group is absent. If they are able to talk, they will ask the teacher where the missing child is. They will also notice and even apparently enjoy seeing another child getting into trouble. Perhaps it is reassuring for them to know that they, who so often transgress, often without knowing why, are not alone. Laughing and giggling does not always indicate pleasure, however. It seems that autistic children giggle when they are apprehensive, as if to reassure themselves.

Even if the teacher at a school for autistic children has not been trained to teach children with autism, the very fact of working with them and them alone, perhaps for several years, means that she will have gained enormous insights into their problems and will have a basic understanding of their handicaps. Moreover, because of their special difficulties the staffing ratios will be high, usually one teacher and classroom helper to every six children. This allows each child to have a little individual attention each day and also means that the teacher has a very good idea of each child's abilities and disabilities. She can arrange the classroom so that there is no material which will distract the restless child and she will have some time to give attention to the child who is withdrawn and solitary.

Teachers of autistic children, too, can and do, like parents, meet and discuss the children's problems and the teaching methods they have found successful. Over the years techniques have been used which have been found to work and slowly a method of teaching is being evolved which new teachers will be able to follow. None of this would happen if autistic children were mixed with others, with different problems.

It may seem that groups of autistic children will merely reinforce each other's isolation, that they will have no one on whom to model their behaviour. This is what usually worries parents and teachers who have not met many autistic children. Most parents, after all, only know their own child well.

Autistic children, because of their very lack of awareness are not usually able to model themselves on others. In their early years especially, they do not appear to notice other children and their first tentative contacts are invariably with adults because interested adults will go more than half way to meet them. Now it may happen that in some schools, there is an interested teacher, who, in spite of having nineteen other children under her care, will yet find time to give extra attention to the autistic child. But parents cannot rely on this and it is not really fair to the others, though parents may stifle their consciences on this point if they are aware of what is happening.

Children who are not severely handicapped and yet are not able to cope in large local authority schools may be able to progress quite well in small private schools. Parents may be able to find a suitable school that will accept the child and the local authority may agree to pay the fees and supply the transport if he is unable to travel on his own. Previously these schools had to be 'recognised' by the Department of Education & Science before a local authority could do this but now the procedure has been changed. These schools are often very satisfactory; they are usually small and the staff are, more often than not, approachable and interested in the problems the children present. It is usual for the child to be seen once a year by the local authority psychiatrist to check that he is progressing. If there is no suitable private school, or school provided by the local authority, then a home teacher may be sent to the child's home. Sometimes a child will have home teaching in the morning and attend the local primary school, with a student or voluntary helper, for a few hours each day. Home tuition may vary from one hour a fortnight, which is hardly helpful, to two hours a day which is considered the same as full time tuition at school.

Some teachers can have very rigid ideas as to what artistic children can or cannot do. They may have read a lot about autism but may not have had much practical experience. Autistic children vary so much, one from the other, that no certain assumptions can be made. Occasionally a teacher who has never met an autistic child before and who has no theories of any sort about the cause or how the child should be taught, works wonders just by observing him and intuitively knowing what to do.

The statutory school leaving age has always been sixteen for handicapped pupils and the raising of the school leaving age for normal children has not changed this. Local authorities may pay for education up to nineteen if they feel that the child is benefiting and courses of further education and training may continue into the early or mid twenties if this is appropriate to the needs of the young person. Most autistic children at Society schools have been allowed education up to nineteen if parents wish it and the school can cope. But what will happen to the children when they leave school? Will local authorities provide anything suitable? The Society, nationally and locally has, as well as two communities, two sheltered workshops—and at one of its schools—a follow on unit for children over school age where they learn the work habits which will be expected of them at the local training centre. Most Society schools have adolescent units where the older school children are taught skills they will need when they leave. But this, though a beginning is a drop in the ocean.

There is one big danger when autistic children are mixed with others, normal or handicapped, and this is their vulnerability. Autistic youngsters, because of their lack of empathy, seldom know how to react to the bully or even the persistent teaser. Their lives can be made a misery and most will not realise that it is within their power to do anything about it; and even if they do, they will probably not try, for fear of retaliation. It is not the least bit of use saying that the autistic youngster must learn to stand up for himself—he won't. It is for this reason that it is unwise to place an autistic child in a school for the maladjusted unless the children are well supervised and the staff are made aware of the dangers. This vulnerability is an integral part of the handicap and will be discussed again as it is important.

If the ideas in the Warnock report are implemented then it seems that as many handicapped children as possible will be educated within the normal school system. However, exceptions will be made for the disturbed and for children needing very special help. This should mean that schools and units for autistic children will remain unaffected. It is possible, though, that there will be a greater tendency not to 'label' a child. If special provision lessens, then this tendency to 'label' may also lessen. Time will tell what the effect will be on the schools and on the future of the children if the report is acted upon. One thing is certain, autistic children are difficult to teach unless they are well supervised so that integration will not be easy.

It would seem that if there is a good school for autistic children available, that this would be the best choice, unless the child is so mildly handicapped that special education is inappropriate. But in spite of this, if a child is happy and getting on well at a school which is not intended for children with his handicap it would be foolish to move him. It is often the people he meets and their willingness to help which matters most in the end.

CHAPTER NINE

Education . . . 2 Academic and Social

It can be argued that every baby is born with a fixed potential and his own temperament and that he will grow up to be the sort of person he was destined to be from the moment of his conception.

It is also argued by many that a child is born as a clean slate and that he is destroyed or made by his education and his environment. The nature/nurture argument.

Both arguments can, and have been advanced after watching autistic children develop from babyhood through childhood and adolescence to adulthood. But the nature argument, with modifications, would seem more likely. It has been shown that the autistic child who, tested when young by someone understanding his handicap, and scoring on a non-verbal IQ test at consistently over 70 will predictably [44, 51] do better in adolescence than an autistic child with a low non-verbal IQ (though it should be stressed that unless the person conducting the IQ test has had experience of the condition, it is perhaps better not attempted). It seems equally likely that little if anything can be done to change the basic temperament or character of the child though it may be possible to modify his behaviour.

This is not to say that parents and teachers should do nothing. Normal children, whatever their potential are educated and whatever the child's temperament parents have to teach him socially acceptable behaviour. The same applies to autistic children with all degrees of handicap although priorities may have to be different. Some will find learning to read or count an impossibility while to others, this may be the one area in which they excel.

No autistic child can really be called socially able as the

global communication problem precludes this. But as with every other aspect of the child's development some autistic children are more sociable than others, just as some are more musical or have more manipulative skill. Those who have more social ability and who are also more academic will be less 'one sided' than those who have an outstanding skill in one area only. It is possible that they will also be less disturbed as it may be this very onesidedness that contributes to the disturbance, at least in the moderately and mildly handicapped. In the severely handicapped it may be that frustration and a complete lack of inner resources plays a very large part in the disruptive behaviour. Again it is important to stress that temperament must make a very great contribution to behaviour. A naturally aggressive or ebullient child will not react in the same way as an anxious, or shy child.

It has been argued that an autistic child who is capable of some academic work should not be taught to read or to do sums as, with his lack of empathy and communication, he is unlikely to enjoy a story or to understand the real use of figures even if he can learn to manipulate them. Instead, it is argued, he should be taught social behaviour. But these skills are not mutually exclusive. Moreover academic teaching is unlikely to fill more than two hours in a fourteen hour day, leaving plenty of time for social training.

Some children are particularly unaware of social situations but may show interest in letters and numbers. It would be extremely foolish to ignore these talents as they may be the only means that parents and teachers have of making any real contact with the child. Social interaction is needed to teach the child academic skills and it may be that it is at these times that the child is first made aware that other people exist. It will be a time that the teacher will want to exploit to the full. There is no guarantee that the time not spent on academic learning will be spent in absorbing social behaviour.

A child does not learn to read purely for pleasure. Written instructions are all around us and so are figures. Nor are these abilities used exclusively for earning a living. They may enrich lives, so that musical talent may be the one consoling feature to a child who has very little else. It would certainly be wrong to try and deny him this interest. Adding columns of figures may seem a useless activity to a person with normal pursuits but to a child who has nothing else at which he excels, this may be a pleasure.

There is a danger, however, that a child with an outstanding skill such as mathematics in the less handicapped or jigsaws in the more severely handicapped may become obsessed with these activities to the exclusion of all else. After all the child is only doing the thing he is good at and if he has a single skill or interest it is not surprising that he should wish to follow this rather than to attempt something that he cannot understand, or at which he is likely to fail. Autistic children seem to be acutely aware of or sensitive to failure [10, 25] and will want to do things that give a feeling of success. This feedback acts as a strong reinforcer and will spur them on to devote even more time to them. It is therefore important to attempt to broaden these areas of interest. If a child has a very marked 'islet' it will be impossible to block entirely even if parents and teachers wanted to. It should, where possible, be channelled into wider and more useful activity. Children with these solitary skills, particularly if they are lacking in social ability are inevitably very strange and it is easy to think that teachers and parents have made them this way. Parents will find that friends who do not understand the condition—and not many do—will think that it is they who have caused the uneven abilities.

Autistic children who have had difficulty in learning become extremely reluctant to move on to anything new, however simple. Even severely handicapped children who seem to be aware of so little appear to be frightened of failure. Others may find enormous enjoyment from studying as, if they have found difficulty in social areas, they may be glad to work at something which is unaffected by the emotions of other people and which remains dependably constant. This may contribute to the absorption in figures or jigsaw puzzles.

It can happen however, that the child will reach a point where he realises he does not understand what is asked of him, reaches a stage where he finds that he is being left behind or that he is 'different' or handicapped and it may be then that he becomes very disturbed, unhappy and refuses to try anything new. Under these circumstances it would seem sensible to consolidate what he already knows and leave him to find his feet again before expecting him to make further progress. Whatever the child is learning, social training should continue and should be part of family life. This is something which needs the co-operation of the whole family as approaches and attitudes must, above all else, be consistent. Social education will include table manners and the family must agree on what they will or will not tolerate. Ideally the child must not find, for instance, that he can get away with snatching at food when his mother is there but not when his father is.

It will be difficult to teach an autistic child social interaction. Usually the more speech a child has the more successful he will be in this area, though there are exceptions. A few children can comprehend much more that they can say and a small number can understand and use gesture.[3, 42] Some children have marked 'islets of intelligence' yet have poor language development and it may not be possible to do more than teach them to be reasonably well behaved in public, to behave politely at table, to learn that they cannot always have their own way and that they must wait their turn with good grace. With the more severely handicapped child even this may not be possible. If the child is not aware of and cannot be made aware of what is expected of him, then he cannot behave in an acceptable manner. The number of children who cannot learn anything useful, however, is low and behaviour modification methods help almost all children if they are consistently applied.

Some children who are not severely handicapped and who learn to speak reasonably well may yet find the three R's difficult. Sometimes they show commonsense in all practical matters and are a great help at home, although their lack of academic achievement may worry them. Others may learn to read early but without much comprehension and may be good at figures, helpful about the house, but never learn to speak fluently, though they will have a basic everyday vocabulary. Again, others though lacking empathy may learn to speak fluently, be very bright academically yet have such poor co-ordination that they will find writing difficult. They may, in fact, find nearly all practical activities beyond them. Much the same mix of abilities and disabilities will be found among the moderately and the severely handicapped (and of course less conspicuously, among normal people also). Even those who learn to speak fluently are still basically noncommunicating as they do not really use speech and gesture in a social context. It seems that the children are just showing the skills, in a distorted form, that they were born with and that autism—the noncommunication and lack of social contact—is a particularly severe handicap superimposed to a greater or lesser extent on the child's natural potential and temperament. These points have been made before but they are worth repeating.

It can be seen that with such very different abilities no one method of teaching can be used, which is one reason why the children benefit from individual attention. However, in spite of their seeming differences, autistic children have in common these difficulties in communicating with and understanding the feelings of other people. Within each school there will be children who have similar abilities and disabilities and teachers with experience will come to recognise and to learn how to teach each group. Autistic children usually cannot take much pressure academically or socially. If they are academically inclined, then this is to be encouraged if it is the only key to their world but it will be necessary to see that they do not become obsessive nor that they are pushed too hard, for they may disintegrate under pressure.

Similarly those with more social skill must be encouraged
to use this. It is, after all, what autistic children most lack.
But one's aims must be realistic. Autistic children do not
really have much feel for social situations; they are very
vulnerable and open to exploitation. They can break down
quite easily if they are expected to cope with too much on
their own. In fact it is safe to say that all pressure must be
relaxed at the first signs of stress.

To return to a point made in a previous chapter it is
interesting that autism seems to affect girls in a different
way. Girls often seem to be more seriously handicapped.
They may become very disturbed as they grow older and are
often harder to control than boys. Little girls are usually
more forward than boys in speech and sociability and in
intuitively understanding the motives of others. Communication may mean more to them. In general they seem
more interested in people than in things, a natural
development in the sex which looks after the family and sees
to its daily needs.

Every human being is born with a certain potential and
temperament and no one suggests that normal children do
not benefit from social training and education. The same is
true of autistic children. As one can never state with absolute
certainty that a child will never learn to read or to understand numbers except in those of low intelligence, then it
would seem sensible to give them all the chance to try but not
to push them if they are incapable of learning. Moreover, if a
child does show an interest in a certain subject such as music
or mathematics, it would be foolish to stop him from
learning because of the fear that he will become obsessional
over it. It may be the one single skill he has which will help
him to develop wider interests and gain some self-respect.
And how can a teacher know what an autistic child of six will
be like at sixteen? She must try and develop any skill that he
shows. He is unlikely to have many and it will be impossible
to tell which will prove to be important to the child ten years
on. It is up to parents and teachers when helping a musically
or mathematically able child to attempt to keep some

balance by introducing other subjects, where possible, and to do their best to stand back and look at the child to see how he appears to others. It is very easy to accept strange behaviour as normal when one is constantly with it.

On the whole autism is a very severe handicap and most children will not be lucky enough to reach the stage where teachers and parents need worry about their musical, scientific or mathematical ability. For the largest number, the most important part of their education will be learning to live with others to the best of their ability.

CHAPTER TEN

Behaviour Modification

The words 'behaviour modification' can raise blood pressure in some people while others believe that it is a certain cure for all handicaps and conditions.

While we have come to understand autism much more over the last twenty years, there has been no real breakthrough in discovering the cause or finding a cure. No one can yet pinpoint the area of the brain which is affected, nor is there a drug which will make the child normal. Apart from a growing awareness of what autism is *not*, little progress has been made into finding what it *is*. We can now describe the children, recognise the handicap when we see it and understand that it is a very severe communication problem. Our teachers too, have learned some appropriate teaching methods but these things have been a gradual realisation, a journey of discovery with the children. The only thing that can be said to have burst upon the scene in recent years is 'behaviour modification'.

As most people know by now operant conditioning/behaviour management/behaviour therapy/behaviour modification are different names for a method of getting people to behave in a more socially acceptable manner by rewarding them when they behave in a way that is deemed 'suitable' and by 'punishing' them when they behave in a socially unacceptable fashion. Perhaps positive and negative reinforcement is a less emotive way of saying reward and punishment.

There is nothing very new in this really. Our Victorian grandparents may not have used this system of child rearing methodically but they did use it and we still do so today though less obviously. When we are pleased by the way our normal children behave we show pleasure, thereby reinforcing that behaviour. And the opposite, too, is true. Behaviour modification works on the same principle but scientifically and consistently applied to produce measurable results. Unwittingly parents may 'punish' good or appropriate behaviour by failing to notice it or by taking it for granted and rewarding bad behaviour by, for instance, paying undue attention to a child in a temper who would be better ignored.[27] Behaviour modification is sensible when one understands its basic aims and most parents are able to learn to apply it or at least to realise when they are wrongly rewarding the child, so that it can become a very useful weapon. It can be used to teach basic skills in the hands of a trained therapist but it does not aim—or claim—to effect a cure.[59] Too much was made of it in its early years and the methods used, especially the 'punishment' could be abused in the wrong hands. It was therefore attacked by many teachers as inhumane.

Because of the particular problems autistic children present—the bizarre behaviour and the lack of communication—behaviour modification is a method of treatment that can be particularly effective in breaking through the barrier of isolation in the first instance and then teaching the child to behave more normally. This makes the child easier to live with, though it in no way cures him. However, as living with an autistic child can be disruptive and disturbing for the whole family this modest aim cannot be ignored.

Because a severely handicapped autistic child lacks communication in any form the 'reward' and 'punishment' have to be primitive, blunt weapons in the first place. A look of displeasure or a smile of encouragement will pass unnoticed when the child lacks eye to eye gaze and in any case cannot interpret facial expression. It will be necessary therefore to use negative reinforcement by denying whatever gives the child gratification and positive reinforcement by hugging the child to make him aware of one's pleasure or displeasure. In the first instance it may be necessary to reward by giving food or better still by something else which is known to give him satisfaction, as he may not a first know that a hug means approval. But as soon as he learns that a smile or a 'good boy' expresses praise and a frown or a firm 'no' disapproval, then physical reinforcement can be phased out. Whenever possible positive rather than negative reinforcement should be used.

There is nothing really new in behaviour modification, it is just a more consistent and more systematic way of doing what parents and teachers normally do.

CHAPTER ELEVEN

The Less Handicapped Autistic Adolescent

This chapter is based on information from research into the 'mildly' handicapped. For some reason, not yet established, there are few girls[3] in this group and only speculation as to why this is so. It is hoped that more will be learned but at the present time is only possible to write with any degree of accuracy on boys.

*   *   *

Although there are many more autistic young people suffering from severe autism a clearer picture of what autism really is emerges when one looks at children who show the symptoms which *must* be present for them to be recognisably autistic yet who do not have all the symptoms that severely handicapped children display.[3, 51] A young person among the least handicapped within this group is able to speak and to understand what is said reasonably well. His speech is likely to be pedantic or irrelevant, it may lack fluency and there may be a tendency to talk 'at' rather than 'to' people so that the to and fro of normal conversation will be lacking.[15] Socially, behaviour is likely to be naïve but will conform to normal peers one is very aware of how different they are and pected academically. Some are exceptionally talented in certain subjects, usually in mathematics or music.

Although these young people are considered 'mildly' handicapped; this is misleading. If compared with their normal peers one is very aware of how differnt they are and the enormous effort they have to make to live in a world where no concessions are made.[22]

The 'mildly' handicapped show much the same symptoms as the severely handicapped but to a lesser degree. Moreover there are some symptoms that are less likely to be seen and these include self injury and stereotyped mannerisms such as the waving of hands beside the face.[4] The children are less likely to show resistance to change, are less likely to develop epilepsy in adolescence[24] and will show fewer deviant social responses. They are more likely to be normally cuddly as babies and to recognise their parents. However they are also more likely to develop complicated rituals and to be more sensitive to sound.[4]

A few of these young people are exceptionally clever but they are best at things which need the minimum of interaction with others, such as music, mathematics or chess; subjects which need no experience of living within a community and which have thrown up child prodigies. They may like watching television, but will not enjoy or understand programmes requiring imagination or identification with the emotions of others. They will prefer documentaries and short comedy programmes and many love music. The less intellectual may prefer soap operas of the 'Star Trek' or 'Dr Who' sort with a familiar characters, plots and signature tunes. The same will apply to books. Hardly ever do they read fiction unless it is to re-read books read to them as children, though they will read to gain knowledge in subjects which interest them.

One group shows an outstanding ability in music; many have perfect pitch. Several have been to music college but they do not seem to be able to use their ability to the full, though a few play the organ at the local church, enjoy going to concerts or listening to records. This may bring them into contact with others with whom they will have something in common. Some have become piano tuners.[58] A few show artistic talent and may be able to draw in perspective from a very early age, without being taught.

Others could, perhaps, learn a craft as they have manipulative and mechanical ability, but this, in practice, has proved difficult to achieve as silversmiths, for instance, take their apprentices at 15 plus. Because of the late social maturation of autistic adolescents it has proved almost impossible for them to get into this kind of job. However some, after doing routine work, may learn a trade such as bricklaying or plumbing.

It is not yet agreed that the children showing the typical Kanner syndrome and those who could be called 'Asperger children' are suffering basically from the same handicap.[58] But there may be a connection.

There seem to be two extremes among the less handicapped. One group shows poor language development but good manual dexterity with basic mathematical and visuo-spatial skills. In childhood this group would have been recognised as having the classic Kanner syndrome.[29] Would these be, perhaps, the designers, craftsmen and engineers of the world if they were not handicapped?

The other group is verbal, though often clumsy and untidy because they are not physically well co-ordinated. They may be brilliant at specific subjects, usually science or economics, though their handwriting may be poor, making the passing of exams difficult. In childhood they might have been recognised as children with the Asperger syndrome.[2] Would these be the scientists and university lecturers? 'Asperger' children do not show the same problem in developing language. Their speech may be delayed but develops normally, with proper sentence construction and an apparent comprehension of the meaning of words and phrases though there may be a tendency to reverse pronouns for a time. Their co-ordination is often poor. However, it may be that 'Asperger' children do not suffer from a sensory aphasia, and that 'Kanner' children do. If this is so then Asberger children perhaps show the purest form of autism? Or are both groups merely showing the extremes of human aptitudes?

Engineers are not always articulate nor do university lecturers necessarily have visuo-spatial skills. Inherited traits may be more easily traced in autistic children. Because of the narrowness of their world they canalise their intelligence into the subject at which they show proficiency and their predominance in this is all the more obvious.

It would be easy to see the members of these two groups as having two distinct handicaps if only people from each group were seen. However, if one takes a large group of young autistic people with normal non-verbal intelligence there is a gradation and an overlap of abilities between one group and the other, the majority falling between the two extremes, some showing, perhaps, verbal ability and good co-ordination, while others show neither but are recognisably autistic with normal non-verbal intelligence. In spite of their differences both groups share the basic problems; no intuitive 'feel' for communication causing a lack of social awareness and a severe lack of empathy. Although one group is verbal, speech is pedantic and factual and conversation on a to and fro everyday level is absent or is apt to be irrelevant or repetitive. Both groups are uninterested in fiction[22, 58] or in television plays requiring identification with the characters. Neither understands innuendo nor do they see themselves as others see them so that their gait, stance and dress may be somewhat odd and their behaviour eccentric. Both groups are inflexible, lack spontaneity and are happiest when they have a fixed daily routine.

Less handicapped young people, far from talking too little, may talk too much.[15] They are unlikely to read the clues which show when the listener is bored or in a hurry, so they will continue to say what they intended to say when they began to speak. They will be very literal and this can cause amusement; they will not understand irony, innuendo or subtlety—language will truly be a rather blunt instrument in spite of the large vocabulary some of them accumulate. It may take them a little while to 'process' what they hear, so that their reactions may be delayed.

To get by, the autistic person has to live by rules. It is not surprising, therefore, that he remains pedantic, inflexible and lacking in empathy. He will have no understanding of changeable relationships. Even autistic young people who have university degrees are dunces when it comes to everyday living. It is interesting to note what Ronald

Englefield has to say about the 'learned response' on page 116.

Autistic people are not necessarily 'loners'. Their attempts at sociability are poorly rewarded.[14] They may enjoy company but are apt to bore their contemporaries with repetitive conversation, irrelevant comments and general lack of social knowhow. Many long for a girlfriend and are unable to understand their failures. Some may have been rejected or teased by an 'in' group that they admire or wish to join and this can cause distress. A few may realise that they have no friends. But on the whole autistic people have difficulty in judging the depths of relationships and are apt to think that anyone who speaks kindly to them is a friend so that they may not be so lonely as one would expect.[15] However they are naïve and immature and their behaviour can be very embarrassing to their brothers and sisters who may go through a stage where they will not wish to invite their friends home.

Odd fears may cling. A fear of dogs is very common and a fear of this sort may prevent even a quite mildly handicapped person from working as he may be afraid to walk down a certain road where he knows that there is likely to be a dog which barks or snaps at his ankles. Parents will have to watch for these fears and do their best to eradicate them before the child leaves school.

One rather lovable trait that autistic people show is a complete disregard for social status. They are unlikely to be able to distinguish between friends whom one treats informally and those who expect, or to whom one feels obliged to give, the red carpet treatment. They may not understand why some people are known as Jane and Harry while others remain as Mr. and Mrs. Johnson. They will be unable to change their accent or behaviour to fit in with the people they are with and for this reason, will stand out less if they remain with people of their own social background.[15]

It seems that some in this group are worried about themselves and are afraid of doing wrong. They appear to be more than ordinarily interested in crime and may question their parents closely about police, prison and court procedure. It is as if they are afraid that they may find themselves involved in some way not of their own volition. A number of parents have remarked how interested their son is in listening to the news for a report of a murder or a breakout from prison and the next day will be the first to get to the paper to read about it. It is probable that they have found themselves in trouble for doing something that they had not realised was wrong. This will have made them wary and afraid of transgressing inadvertantly. Autistic youngsters are very law abiding and seldom wish to kick over the traces. Others are interested in hospitals and accidents, probably for a similar reason. They sometimes worry about falling ill or dying. It seems difficult for them to see these natural events in perspective.

Some show an unwillingness to throw anything away. It is as if by getting rid of familiar objects they also lose their sense of security. Parents may have to resort to removing things by stealth or by insisting outright that very old or useless objects are discarded before their house begins to resemble a junk yard. The autistic person living an independent life may not have anyone to supervise him and his flat or rooms may become more and more congested as he grows older. Little paths to necessary items of living equipment will be left open and it may be that in spite of the surrounding chaos he will neatly lay a place for himself at the corner of the dining room table, just as his mother did many years before.

Religion may play an important role in the autistic person's life.[17] There are probably several reasons for this. It is reliable; the services occur at the same place and at the same time every week. It is conventional, approved of and he will meet the same people whom he will think of as his friends. It will also provide social ocasions in which he can join and where his eccentricities will be accepted by the other parishioners. Some may not find spiritual belief difficult and may be strengthened and comforted while others may never understand the spiritual message. But the music, the familiar prayers and the quiet and ordered atmosphere will probably please them and help them to feel secure. Moreover its teachings provide a moral code, a structure and discipline from without, which they so badly need. Autistic young people are unsure of themselves and worry about doing wrong and the certainty that religion provides is of great help to them. This is almost always true of the more orthodox religions, with their ceremony, ritual and language, which, though beautiful, is remote. The more evangelical churches and the new religions with their emphasis on hellfire and damnation or the too literal interpretation of the Bible may be frightening to them. However, an advantage as far as parents are concerned is that if the autistic person manages to live an independent life after their deaths, then, should anything happen to him the members of the congregation are likely to notice and to help. In a small village any deviation from the normal routine will probably be noticed but within the anonymity of a suburb or large town this cannot be taken for granted.

How many autistic people will be able to live independent lives? Though it is too soon to say for certain it is unlikely that there will be very many. Much will depend on temperament. An autistic person may, in spite of his eccentricities, hold down a job. He will learn to pay the bills; he may indeed be meticulous over this. He will learn to budget and to cook but he will probably not have a varied diet. He will eat the food he has been taught to prepare but he is unlikely to experiment. He may hoard. He is not likely to notice that his coat is grubby or out of fashion, though he will take care to button it neatly. He will live to a strict routine and may be thought eccentric by his neighbours. However, in spite of all this, he will manage. He may not be unhappy. To be unhappy one has to be aware of what one is missing and some autistic people do not appear to know that they are different.[22]

But many do realise that they have problems although some adjust philosophically to the handicap. Parents report that they are pleasant to live with and many have a good, though unsubtle sense of humour. Others are unhappy young men who know that they have great difficulties and are very anxious and depressed. Some parents tell their child that he is autistic and explain what it means, others may tell him that he has certain problems but do not give them a name. Some parents may prefer to say nothing. This is a decision that can only be made by parents. If they sense that their child is worried about himself, then it may help him to know and to understand that it is not his fault that he is different.

The autistic young person is not competitive and may not notice that his peers are overtaking him. When he does wake up to this he may feel deeply inadequate. Acute anxiety or breakdown may occur when he changes his job or moves house and has to abandon one set of rules and routines for another. He does adjust—given patience and understanding, but it will take time. A similar reaction may occur when something changes at his place of work. He may find it difficult or impossible to explain why he is upset so that his behaviour will not be understood by his employer or his colleagues.[22] The worry over moving house seems more common in the older less handicapped person. As children they are unlikely to be very concerned.

Some autistic young men, usually those who are at the lower end of this ability range, will attend the local Adult Training Centre for the mentally handicapped sometimes only for a few years until they are mature enough to find outside employment. Some leave university, art or music college with high qualifications which they are unable to use fully because of their handicap and resulting personality problems. Parents may be blamed for overeducating them. However, it is difficult to see what else they could have done. In the first place, the young person may have found that his only talent lay in passing examinations and he may wish to study to achieve the rewarding glow of success. He may have no social or manual skills which could have been developed to any great degree and so would have remained unemployable even if he had been dissuaded from studying. If his skills were in art or music, then, even if he were unable to work in these fields, his trained talent would have given him great pleasure and may have possibly been used for earning a living at a later stage in his life.

When work is scarce, even a bright autistic school leaver of 17 or 18 years old may not be able to find employment. He, or his parents, may decide that, rather than hang around at home, a course at a polytechnic or college of further education will not only give him a semi-sheltered environment for a little longer but may also teach him a useful skill. Moreover, when the time comes for him to leave, the employment situation may have improved. There is a danger, though, that the young man will expect to find work to match his qualifications [15] and in some cases it may upset him to see those less qualified overtaking him. Parents will have to try to make him aware that it may not be possible for him to work to his potential because of his special problems. However, as he is unlikely to be able to understand a point of view other than his own, this will not be easy. A lot will depend on his temperament. By the very nature of the handicap there is not likely to be a fail-safe decision for parents to take.

In fact, the all embracing handicap suffered by these young people, apart from their 'aloneness' is their lack of empathy. They have immense difficulty in seeing anyone's point of view but their own and may blame their parents for all their problems. [22]

Parents of the less handicapped may have the satisfaction of knowing that their child is not severely affected but they are beset with uncertainties for the future. When he leaves school he may find work, but his parents, aware of his dependence, realise that he will have to live a normal life without the safety net of being recognised as handicapped. With them in the background ready to step in there may be no problems, but what happens when this no longer obtains? This is why some parents may look around for a suitable sheltered community. The kind of life a young man leads depends partly on his abilities, how vulnerable he is, his parents' wishes, his own wishes and the facilities available to him.[22] He may be rebellious and obstinate and insist on doing academic studies against his parents' better judgement and the less handicapped he is the less likely he is to take their advice.

It seems that 'mildly' handicapped autistic people are doomed to spend their lives figuratively climbing a mountain. At each stage a little more of the view is revealed to them. They continue to learn and their horizons widen and as they do so, the 'islets of intelligence' which were such a feature of their early years are likely to diminish or disappear. Are they ever able to look around and see the whole and not the part?[22] As far as is known at the present time some of the less handicapped have improved remarkably as they have grown and they appear to continue to mature the older they get, but they remain slightly apart— and different.

CHAPTER TWELVE

Adolescence

Adolescence is a trying time for everyone, including the adolescent, as any parent will tell you. There is the danger, too, that any change of behaviour at this age will be attributed to adolescence, so that one must be sure to exclude other factors before being certain that it is this that is causing the problem.

There are fewer autistic girls.[34] Adolescence is sometimes more stormy for them and their families may find them very difficult to handle. Others manage to survive without any great degree of disturbance. Severely handicapped girls have more difficulty in coming to terms with the maturation of their bodies than boys, because of the much greater intrusion this has on their lives. For this reason many autistic girls have been put on the pill.

Boys may or may not have problems. Some seem to sail through these years without too much turmoil yet other parents report that they almost gave up in despair because their son became rebellious, aggressive and destructive.

It is obvious, but it can be forgotten, that the young people grow large, often very suddenly and that aggression from a sixteen year old is much more frightening than the same aggression from a ten year old.[44] Similar factors apply to rebelliousness and destructiveness. A mother can deal if necessary by force, with a rebellious eight to ten year old and any destructive tendencies at this age will be as nothing compared to the havoc a sixteen year old can wreak.

Parents expect to have problems at this time with their normal children, so unless one's autistic child is particularly placid, which is not very likely, then it is to be expected that there will be a period of more than usual disruption.

Even if the young person does not become disturbed in the

rebellious, negative way that many do, he may come to realise, at this time, that there is another sex. Many less handicapped autistic adolescents are seemingly unaware of this and remain so—others are attracted but yet do not know how to approach the young person to whom they have taken a fancy.[16] They have not the same social awareness or inhibitions which restrains the normal sixteen year old from going up to a pretty girl to stroke her hair, much as he might like to. As the autistic young man has difficulty in initiating social relationships he will have no idea how to 'chat her up'. Many of the young men will spend their pocket money on household or fashion magazines as these contain photographs of attractive girls.

If the young person is severely handicapped he is likely to be under some form of supervision so it will be the 'mildly' or the moderately handicapped who are more at risk from public misunderstanding. Fortunately few understand innuendo or read fiction for pleasure so that much of today's permissiveness both written and spoken will pass unnoticed. However the same cannot be said for the rather explicit illustrations now allowed in some magazines and in plays on television which pass unremarked, and almost unnoticed, in today's world by normal people.

The more severely handicapped, too, may have sexual urges but these are probably less likely to be directed towards other people. Those who, for instance, masturbate must be taught that this is only acceptable in the privacy of their own room.

It is sad, but it may be easier for everyone if the young man is taught that the opposite sex is not for him. Many people live celibate lives and the forming of day to day relationships, so difficult for those with autism, makes the forming of a sexual relationship seem almost impossible. One can imagine perhaps, a 'mildly' handicapped young man, good looking, good natured and guileless, being attractive to a young girl but she would have to share her life with someone without empathy and therefore seldom able to understand her feelings. She would have to be willing to make the decisions and take most of the responsibility for the day to day running of their marriage. It might work, but though this is possible, it is not likely to happen frequently.

How does one teach an autistic young person who is unable to mix with others that he cannot pat, stroke or stare at every young girl who takes his fancy? It seems to be of little use just to tell him he mustn't. If he is able to live a semi-independent life his parents cannot be with him all the time. It would seem that they must actively teach him how to behave by taking him to places where he will meet young girls—on buses and in shopping centres for instance—and then to intervene every time he attempts to touch, stroke or stare. If there is a relative or friend who would help this is preferable as it is likely that he will pay more attention to them.

This kind of situation is not likely to occur with more severely handicapped young people. It is possible that they will become more disturbed and more difficult to handle. Because they lack inner resources, filling the day for strong, healthy, six foot young men will become a problem. Many enjoy walking and this is certainly what they need, but seldom get, because they have to be accompanied. On the other hand, it is often during this time that the overactive child can change into an underactive adult. The child who could not stay still for a moment may now sit around doing nothing.[44] It may take constant prodding to get him to work at the simplest task. However the child who would not stick at a routine household job when younger may now actively seek work, finding washing up or polishing floors preferable to his previous aimless activity.

A few become anxious rather than rebellious or aggressive and this can become a problem too, especially if they are aware enough to realise that they are different from others.

If parents can cope during these difficult years there is evidence that as their children move into their twenties they do settle down once more, although as yet, no one had had long experience of older autistic people in any number.

One cannot tell parents with certainty what to expect

during these years. They may be relatively trouble free or
there may be storms ahead.

CHAPTER THIRTEEN

Hospitals, Communities, Hostels or Home?

Autism is, in effect, only as old as the bulk of the early membership of the Society. There are a few middle aged and elderly people who were never diagnosed but whose behaviour is recognisably autistic. They are people who are less handicapped and have managed to stay within the community and, as well as these, there are adult autistic young people who were among the first to be diagnosed. But by far the largest number is now the young adolescent and school leaver and those born during the last fifteen years. So it is only recently that provision for the future has been seriously considered. It is difficult to provide facilities in advance, sensible as this would be, as the problems are really not understood clearly until the needs arise.

The NSAC has not had the same clear cut idea on what form 'care' should take as it had on 'education'. This is not surprising when one considers that by 16–18 years, everyone has a far more realistic idea of what their child will be able or not able to achieve. Many will spend their lives in a hospital for the subnormal and others will stay at home until both parents die or become too old to care for them. A few will be able to work within the community with supervision, perhaps living in a hostel and working in a normal job or in a sheltered workshop. Some parents will seek the safety of a community for mixed handicaps if they feel that their child will be unable to cope with the outside world. There is now a community run by the NSAC which takes up to forty young autistic people and a local Society has bought a property in the north west of the country and has provided a community for autistic people from that area. The National Society and local Societies are now also beginning to open training centres known as LEAP projects (Life Education for Autistic

People), either on a day or a weekly boarding basis. But long term care is in its infancy and it will be several years before it is known whether the arrangements that are now being made are best. It is likely that there is no 'best'. Some places will be more suitable than others for some autistic people.

It seems that as the handicap varies so widely in degree, the temperaments of the young people and the preferences of the parents are so different, a number of separate approaches is probably an advantage. Where the young person is able to make use of facilities provided by the authorities for those with different handicaps, then this is ideal and in many cases this is possible so that there is no problem. However, there are always a few who remain apart and difficult to place whatever their degree of handicap and it is this group and how best they can be fitted into the varying facilities, or how these facilities could be arranged to suit them better, which needs consideration.

Mental subnormality hospitals where many are obliged to go, either because they are too disruptive at home or because their parents can no longer care for them and there is nowhere else, may be good or bad, depending very much on the area in which the families live. Unfortunately there is seldom any choice so that if parents are not satisfied with the local hospital they will have to move to a different catchment area and this may not always be easy or even possible. The alternative is to make a fuss and some are not able to do this.

The disaffection with hospital provision seems to stem from two main sources. One is the staff/patient ratio and the other is frequent staff changes on wards. Autistic people, especially the most severely handicapped, have few inner resources and if they are fortunate enough to attend the hospital workshop—and this can by no means be taken for granted—they are left, apart from mealtimes, from 4.30 until bedtime and all the weekend, with nothing to do. Because the severely handicapped cannot amuse themselves or integrate with others, they may use this time to shred up the bedclothes, sit rocking on their beds or by injuring themselves—this last, it appears, is better than doing nothing. The overworked staff are not likely to be able to do very much to help. Moreover when they do find time to intervene and some sort of rapport between nurse and patient is established, staff are likely to be moved to a different ward and the whole process begins again.

People who work in hospitals are compassionate people and do what they can. Autistic people *are* difficult, so what is the answer? Unfortunately one way to deal with the problem is to sedate the young person very heavily and this is sometimes necessary if he is very overactive and a danger to the physically and mentally handicapped residents with whom he may have to share a ward. (But again, like the younger child, why is it that the disruptive and robust are sometimes expected to share the same quarters as the frail and disabled?) Or he may need to be put under restraint to stop him from injuring himself or disturbing others. Both these 'answers' to the problem are painful for the parents if they are alive—but they may dread even more thinking of what may happen when they are dead and are no longer able to exert any influence.

Although it is easy and popular to find scapegoats, no one is to blame for this situation (though each time parents have reason to feel that their child is being poorly cared for, this will have to be investigated) nor does it necessarily arise. Those who are less handicapped or more sociable are not so likely to be affected in this way. They will be able to join the outings and take part in the entertainments arranged by the hospital staff. Most of the young people are cared for and are content but parents are aware that things can go wrong and would like to know whether anything can be done. Surprisingly, sometimes it may be almost impossible to get a severely disturbed young person *into* hospital. Parents may be desperate but in certain areas there is a shortage of beds. The more efficiently a family is seen to cope the less likely they are to get a place for their child.

There is one heartening change of attitude that has come about within the last ten years and this is the willingness of

young people to offer help to charities by working volun-
tarily with the handicapped. Even if each person who
volunteered would give an hour of his time every week to taking an autistic person from the ward and walking him round
the usually extensive hospital grounds, this alone would do
much to mitigate the problem. Most autistic people are
healthy and strong and love to walk but who, working in a
hospital, has time to accompany them? But hospitals, too,
could make an effort. Surely it would be better to harness
surplus energy by using it to dig up some of those extensive
grounds for growing vegetables? A Saturday morning spent
digging is surely beter than a Saturday morning spent
rocking on a bed.

It seems that a great deal of time is wasted in arguing that
a community in the country is better than one in a town or
city or vice versa. But who can say? It is likely that this
depends more on the parents' views than on their child's and
in any case the well-being a community generates is far more
likely to depend on the staff than on its position. As far as is
possible there should be communities in both town and
country—and 'country' does not necessarily mean fifteen
miles from the closest neighbour but in or near a village with
a market town within easy reach. In these days of expensive
travel, it would be sensible not to be too far from civilisation.

Many more of the young people than already do so could
work in Adult Training Centres if these were a little more
tolerant of the autistic person's odd behaviour.[7] There are
several ways of dealing with this and all could be tried.
Someone with a knowledge of autism should be recruited, as
a member of staff, to work in a training centre which has
several autistic people, or the NSAC should, as it is
beginning to do, open training centres of its own where
possible. While parents are still vigorous, or their son or
daughter is not too difficult, then he or she can return home
daily, eventually and by easy stages, learning to live in the
local hostel. Another approach is to train the young people
at a special centre, when they leave school, to work in the
local authority training centre. The staff employed to teach

them would also learn a lot and they could teach the staff who are already at, or who plan to work at, training centres. Some autistic youngsters leave school, work at the training centre, live at the local hostel and have few problems.

The small number of autistic people who find normal employment are scattered all over the country. Some know that they are autistic, others know that they are 'different', while others seem unaware that they have problems. They are solitary people as one would expect, not necessarily from choice but because they do not know how to integrate. In most cases they are very vulnerable and parents worry for the time when they will have to manage as best they can without their support. Fortunately the young people continue to learn and although they remain odd they do improve in competence over the years. It seems that a few go through a very difficult phase in their late teens or early twenties before they adjust to their problems and, of these, some will need psychiatric treatment. This appears to be a phase as far as it is possible to tell at the present time.

As with the autistic school child, many people think it is wrong to put autistic people together in a community. Again it is felt that the friendliness of the person with Down's syndrome complements the autistic person's isolation. But so much depends on the individual. Each autistic person is different and it is impossible to generalise. Some are particularly vulnerable and are easily made the butt of the resident bully and are therefore happier in a more protected environment. It is unlikely in any case that communities which care for the mentally handicapped will wish to take many autistic people, especially if they are noncommunicating and disturbed. They are likely to accept only those who fit their system and the young people they choose would probably fit equally well into the local adult training centre and hostel or be the very kind of young person which a community for autistic people needs to help make it a viable proposition.

Some of the young people live at home with their parents and this can suit everyone. The parents receive an allowance which in some cases includes an extra payment for looking after a handicapped person who needs constant attention day and night or a slightly lower allowance for constant attention during the day. Parents may be pleased to have their child with them, thus ensuring his well-being, but they may dread the future as they fear that he will not be satisfactorily placed after their deaths and would like to see him settled.

There should be flexibility so that if the choice the parents make turns out to be wrong, there are alternatives.[7] Today this is not usually so and it is this which worries parents more than anything else. Autism is one of the most difficult of handicaps, whether it is severe or mild, for both the victim and his parents.

CHAPTER FOURTEEN

The Autistic Family

There is a danger that parents with an autistic child in the family will either pay undue attention to the handicapped member, or go to the other extreme and not give him the attention he needs. Balancing the emotional requirements of the various members of the family is extremely difficult and parents will have to try to step outside themselves and see the situation objectively.

It is quite unfair to other members of the family and will breed resentment overt or covert, if the autistic child is allowed to dictate how the household is run. Yet, for the sake of peace it is only too easy to give in to him by letting him have his own way; letting him take and destroy his brother's toy, knowing that to intervene will mean an hour's tantrum; letting his behaviour ruin a much looked forward to outing. These events will be inevitable on some occasions but if the family is to stick together and come to no emotional harm then an effort will have to be made to control the autistic child's behaviour. If this is possible and in most cases it is, then in the long run it is kinder because the child will be able to remain within his family if not for good, then for a little longer. This control has to begin early, before the child can understand the reason. Indeed some autistic children will never understand why climbing on to furniture is unacceptable. However, it is better for them to find that this is not welcome while they are still small. Behaviour which is acceptable in a three year old will be frowned on by everyone by the time the child is eleven.[18]

It is probably simpler for parents if the autistic child is the youngest in the family or is of a different sex from the other. It is easier to make excuses for the behaviour of the youngest child that are acceptable to his brothers and sisters and if the

child is of a different sex, then differences in handling and
comparisons of behaviour are not so obvious. If the autistic
child is the first, the other children, before they are old
enough to understand, may resent the way he can apparently get away with things that they know very well
would be forbidden them should they try to emulate him. If,
occasionally they express resentment, or even say they hate
their brother, parents should not be shocked. It is better that
they should be able to express their usually fleeting feelings
openly. It is far better that they should do this than take it
out on the handicapped child when the parents are not
around to protect him.

It is very easy for the parents to give the autistic child
more than his fair share of attention. He is very unaware of
danger and so dependent—and because he looks bright and
attractive it seems that there must be a key which will unlock
some compartment of the brain and so cure him. There are
some parents who will find the truth difficult or even
impossible to face so that in spite of all evidence to the
contrary, and whatever they are told, they will not admit
even to themselves, how seriously the child is handicapped.
Parents may say 'If only I could get through to him, he'd be
normal', not realising that getting through to a child with a
global communication handicap is no simple problem. On
the whole, however, the majority of parents are realistic and
objective enough to assess their child very accurately.
Mostly they hope for little more than that he should reach
his potential and be happy.

Although the other children will soon realise that their
brother is not normal, they may not realise what is wrong
with him. If he is not severely handicapped parents may not
wish to have him labelled, especially if they live in a small
community and they feel that he is acceptable as he is. They
may feel that to have him known as autistic is to stigmatise
him. The wheel has turned, so that many people think that
all autistic children are very severely handicapped when
fifteen years ago they believed they were all geniuses. On the
other hand it may help the child to know that he is autistic

and it is not his fault that he is different from others—and it may help his brothers and sisters to understand him better too. Some parents may prefer to be less specific and to explain his difficulties to him—and to his relatives—as a communication problem. It will be for his parents to decide. They will know his temperament and the environment in which he is living.

The majority of families with autistic children will not have this problem as their child will be more severely handicapped and he will be described quite openly as autistic. Although he will also be mentally handicapped some parents may prefer him to be known as autistic. This will describe his behaviour, though, in fact, autism is a far more serious problem than the accompanying mental deficiency.

As the brothers and sisters grow up they may become extremely sensitive. They may not want to be seen in public with their autistic brother, but this stage is usually outgrown and many brothers and sisters become the child's best protector and advocate. When the children are young, too, they may be the only ones who really understand their handicapped brother or sister and this may hold true throughout their lives.

Parents will have to make sure that their other children, as well as getting their full share of attention and love, also receive due encouragement and that their achievements are noted and praised. Some parents may find it difficult not to overcompensate. Occasionally the others are poorly disciplined as parents feel that they have rather a lot to put up with. Children, however, do not appear to resent limits on their freedom if these are seen to be fair and no more severe than their contemporaries, but parents must make sure that they are properly rewarded and thanked for any help they give. It is essential that a little of the parents' time should be devoted just to them, without their handicapped brother or sister.

Because of their lack of inner resources, autistic children seem happier living within a disciplined home. As they grow older, if not too severely handicapped, they may prefer doing housework, cutting the grass or cleaning the car. The alternative to work of this kind is often to revert to obsessions or to do nothing at all.

The parents' biggest worry as they grow older is almost certainly the future of their autistic child. Some parents will prefer to find residential placement early and so see their son or daughter settled. Other parents will want to keep their child at home as long as possible. They will probably not wish to burden the brothers or sisters with the responsibility of caring for him as they will have their own lives to lead. Sometimes a brother or a sister will offer to act as guardian or trustee and, as he or she will be likely to understand him better than anyone else, parents will be grateful for the offer. However, not every autistic child has a brother or sister or a brother or sister living in this country—or perhaps one wishing to take on the responsibility. Most will not know what the facilities are, nor the entitlements and rights of the autistic person, nor will every brother or sister understand the handicap.

For this reason the National Society has devised an advisory scheme. Briefly the idea is to provide a 'godparent' or guardian (the parent of an autistic child—or a person who has taught autistic children) who will watch over an autistic person once his parents have died. With the NSAC in the background to give advice, he or she will be able to advise those who are looking after the autistic person who may not understand the reasons for his behaviour. It could happen that when the parents are no longer there to protect him he will run into difficulties. He may go through a crisis, such as eviction from a hostel or confinement to a side ward of a hospital. If there is someone to stand by him, to take a personal interest and fight on his behalf, then the future will not seem so bleak.

CHAPTER FIFTEEN

Aggression—and the autistic person

The autistic child can be violent under some circumstances but violence directed towards other people supposes that the child is aware of others and not only feels anger, resentment or jealousy but can pinpoint the person who has aroused this feeling. When young, autistic children are not very aware of other people and they are usually 'violent' in a non-specific manner. During a temper tantrum for instance they may hit or bite whoever is standing by them or they may throw objects across rooms or out of windows without a thought for the probable consequences. A child whose obsession was joining up 'pop on' beads and swinging the resulting string round his head would give any child who walked within his orbit a nasty blow, but this would be in no way calculated. Yet autistic children, who can often be hurt by the actions of other autistic children, do not fear them as they may learn to fear the bully. It is not until the autistic child has developed consciousness of people as individuals who may thwart his wishes that he will attack and even when he has reached this stage of development, powerful inhibitions may stop him from taking this step. Although one cannot say that an autistic child or young person will never purposely attack another person, it is more usual for the autistic person to be the one who is attacked.'

It seems probable that the very severely handicapped may never become sufficiently aware of others to direct violence towards them though they will hit out when they are frustrated or angry. However, one cannot minimise the dangers of this. If one has seen a two year old in a rage, red in the face with arms and legs flailing and then imagines this behaviour in a six foot eighteen year old, the consequences cannot be brushed aside even though the aggression is undirected. The less handicapped, though, are very well aware of the retaliation that may follow any aggression on their part. They suspect, rightly, that they will be unable to cope with it and are therefore inhibited from taking action.

It is probable that autistic children who have shown a tendency to attack others are to be found within the moderately handicapped group, because it is within this group that the children have developed sufficiently to understand that other people may stop them from doing things that they want to do and yet may not fear, or may not be placed in situations where they will be inhibited from, attacking people they see as restricting or teasing them. Children within this group will usually be under some kind of supervision and will not have to attempt to defend themselves in the outside world.

There are exceptions to every rule and autistic children with all degrees of handicap may show tendencies to violence. Some of the severely handicapped can become violent in adolescence and may need heavy sedation. But it seems that the less handicapped who are living within the community are very unlikely to show violence and are, in fact, very vulnerable. By the very way they walk, stand or wear their clothes they signal to street gangs that they are different and likely targets for a bit of fun. Because of their lack of empathy and contingent social ineptitude, they may have no idea of how to cope with circumstances such as these. It would seem too large a task to attempt to recreate every situation they may be called upon to face so as to teach them how to react to it. It may be simpler to warn them not to wander alone, especially in the evenings and to avoid certain areas. Even so, unless they live in a protected environment they may have to face situations where they are the obvious quarry for those who enjoy teasing. This group can, however, show aggression at home, because they know that their parents will not retaliate.

Parents of autistic children are distressed when their son or daughter comes home with scars or bruises. Severely disturbed young people in hospital are sometimes placed in one ward and because hospitals for the mentally subnormal are not well staffed, they lack supervision and may injure themselves through boredom, or perhaps each other, usually unintentionally. It is not so likely that they will be the butt of bullies, even when they are in the community. Bullies get satisfaction from bullying someone who is aware and therefore afraid of them. Also gangs find it more entertaining to tease someone who can be relied upon to say something inept and therefore 'amusing'. It is for these reasons that many parents seek some form of protection for their child, even if in other respects he is capable of living a normal life.

It is worth repeating that because they are so vulnerable autistic children should not be placed in schools for the maladjusted child. It is not possible to say that this has never been shown to work but the two conditions are very different and need two opposing forms of treatment. A child who is maladjusted needs a long rein, an informal atmosphere. An autistic child needs to know where he is and therefore needs a structured environment. The two methods are incompatible. Moreover, the autistic child has very little idea of how to defend himself from teasing and bullying. The teacher, considering the needs and emotions of the maladjusted child may well be pleased when he loses his inhibitions and begins to tease another child. Teachers of maladjusted children are trained to encourage quite different qualities from those who teach autistic children.

Although no controlled studies have been undertaken it does seem that autistic girls are more difficult (See Part II Chapter 3). Is it because girls are possibly more interested in or aware of other people than boys that they appear to show more directed violence towards them? It seems that even quite severely handicapped girls are aware when others are thwarting their wishes and they may attack the person they see as being responsible. It may be this ability, this awareness of others, which makes some girls more difficult to handle and not premenstrual tension, so often blamed before most severely handicapped girls were put on the pill.

CHAPTER SIXTEEN

Doctor-Parent Relationship

Even today certainly not all GP's, paediatricians, community doctors or child psychiatrists recognise autism. Because the handicap can seem so very different in different children and because it is comparatively rare (approximately 4 per 10,000 of school age children will suffer from it and only half of these will have it in its 'pure' form[34]) it is not always easy to get a diagnosis. There are other reasons, too. Some doctors prefer not to diagnose because they do not think that giving a child a label is helpful. It is difficult to understand why there is this dislike of labelling. It may be that the doctors feel that as there is no cure then giving the handicap a name is of no assistance. They may think that parents would be happier not knowing what is wrong or they may not be sure that the child is autistic. Most parents prefer to be given the facts, however, and to make up their own minds. If the child is autistic but not diagnosed the parents would not consider joining the Society where they would get information and the chance to meet other parents. The local authority would not provide a school or class as it would not be aware that there were any children needing this service, nor would the child be sent to an independent boarding school for autistic children. It is easy to see the towns and cities in the United Kingdom where autism is diagnosed because of the number of special schools there are in these areas. Even the NSAC finds it difficult to open a day school in a place where autism is not readily diagnosed.

There are also a few doctors, a diminishing number happily, who say that there is no such handicap; that like dyslexia it is a label invented for middle class parents who cannot face the fact that they have a retarded child.

A GP might well have an excuse for thinking this. He is

not likely to meet many autistic children—perhaps one or two in all his years of practice—but doctors working in hospitals where these children are likely to be referred should by this time be aware that there is a group of children who, though of varying temperament and ability, yet show very similar characteristics, the most outstanding being their isolation from others, lack of normal speech and bizarre behaviour. This behaviour and the abnormalities of speech are very consistent and as the children usually live several miles apart, they can not have copied each other. Their lack of communication in any form and its resulting isolation should be apparent to anyone skilled in the observation of childhood behaviour.

If the doctor is not certain he should refer the child to someone who is more experienced in this field and tell the parents what he suspects. Parents do not expect doctors to know everything and will not think any the less of him if he admits that he does not know very much about the handicap and that he may be wrong.

However, most doctors do what they can. There is a tendency in this country for doctors to be very reticent. Meeting people from overseas it is amazing to hear how much they are told. Perhaps our doctors are unduly non-committal? To understand a condition is usually to fear it less.

A great deal depends on how parents are told of their child's handicap. So much unhappiness is caused by doctors who, because of their own poor communicative skill, lack of empathy or embarrassment are unable to tell parents in a way that they can understand and in a manner that is sympathetic, what is wrong with the child. Sometimes they are abrupt, suggesting that the parents should forget the child, 'put him away' and have another or parents may be asked to come back in six months without being given any information at all. Parents are confused and anxious when they know their child is handicapped but are told nothing.[54] They may be told that the child is autistic and that he will never recover but no one explains what is meant by 'recover'. However busy doctors are they should be able to spend ten minutes with the parents. The parents will, through their daily lives, have picked up a great deal of misinformation and a number of attitudes towards any form of mental deviation and they will need someone to explain the implications and to dispel the fears that having such a child will mean. They will also want to know what problems they are likely to meet. As the parents will not be able to absorb all the information at one time it should be possible for them to see the specialist twice within the first month and not have to wait six months before they see him again. They are certain to think of things that they should have asked and will need to know almost as soon as they have closed the consulting room door after their first visit.

Parents need to be told the truth. It has been shown that IQ tests, given by a psychologist experienced with autistic children, are a remarkably accurate predictor of the likely development of the child [33, 37] so that it is possible to tell which autistic children are likely to progress and which are not. But most hospitals are not yet experienced enough to do this. Parents should therefore be told that a few autistic children will learn to lead independent or semi-independent lives though remaining slightly odd and that others, though moderately retarded may yet learn some useful skills. However they must be told that more than half are severely retarded but that, even so, most can be helped to live with their own families during their childhood if this is what parents want. Many ways are being devised for teaching simple skills. These help the parents and give the children a sense of achievement. The NSAC runs an Information and Advisory Service which will help the parents to find where the schools are and will put them in touch with those who have experience in this field.

It is at this stage that the parents need all the assistance they can get. Social workers who understand the problem can be a support to a family but not many social workers employed by local authorities have much knowledge of the handicap. Why should they? They are trained to deal with a wide variety of problems and autism is not one they will come across very often. They may have heard that it is a condition brought about by faulty upbringing and if they think this, then it would be better if they did not visit, for they will be likely to take away what little confidence the parent has in the daily handling of her child. Frequently mothers tell of trying to watch an overactive child, while at the same time do the ironing and make the social worker a cup of tea. The Social worker may sit down for a chat and expect the mother to do the same. Mothers have said how it would be helpful if the social worker watched the child and did the ironing thus allowing them time to catch up on their disorganised household duties.

It is not uncommon for the mother to know far more than the social worker, not only about autism but about the local facilities. If the social worker would make an effort before visiting the family, to find out as much as possible about the handicap and about suitable special schools, or if she can put the family in touch with other parents, perhaps through the local society for autistic or mentally handicapped children then she will be welcome. She may advise on ways that the mother can teach the child to feed himself or use the lavatory. If so, she will be very welcome indeed. Or, if she will listen without criticising, watching the child perhaps while the mother works, this too, will help. As most social workers are not trained to understand autism (as mentioned above, it would hardly be worthwhile as they will meet so few children) then this is all that can reasonably be expected. Not all parents suffer from feelings of guilt, though most social workers seem to expect them to. Most are just overwrought from hard work and need help. However, it has not been the intention to find fault with social workers. It is just that they have more opportunity than most to affect directly the parents' attitudes, their fears and their hopes. It is therefore important that they have some understanding of the problems faced by families. Fortunately social workers know much more now than in the early days.

Doctors and hospital staff too, should listen to what

parents say. Parents may not know much about the functioning of the brain but they do know their own child; things that the doctor could not possibly know from seeing a child for half an hour every six months. If they say that he will not sit on a stool without a back rest to take a hearing test, they are likely to be right and time will not be needed to take him on a second occasion as the first test was 'screamed off'. Parents on their six monthly visits dread finding that they are to see a different doctor, an occurrence which happens not infrequently. Although each doctor has the case notes the parents may be asked to go right back to the beginning each time—sometimes even being asked the child's name and date of birth.

It is unusual now for psychiatrists to suggest to parents that a course of psychoanalysis would help. But when it was believed that parents caused the handicap they found themselves under scrutiny too. They had the feeling that every word they said and every movement they made was being checked. If they were forthcoming then this would indicate a flaw in their character which would have affected the child and if they were reticent, this too would have had an unfavourable effect on him. If the psychiatrist is looking for certain behavioural traits he will almost certainly find them and parents will sense this even if nothing is said.

Many children do go to play therapy though, usually at the child guidance clinic or family health centre. Young autistic children seldom benefit for the reasons the therapist expects. The child will have no imagination and will not work out his supposed inhibitions in sand and water play or by being talked to, as he is unlikely to understand what is being said, moreover his behaviour will be very uninhibited. But he may benefit marginally from getting an hour or so of someone's undivided attention. However, an older autistic child who has developed a rudimentary imagination, has some grasp of language and who has some special problem will, perhaps, profit from the experience in the way expected of him.

Although parents will welcome an opportunity to speak to

the specialist, a visit to hospital with a young autistic child is not easy, especially if other children have to be taken too. Mothers often have to cope on their own as the child's father will be working and travelling by public transport followed by a long wait in an out patients' department can be a nightmare.

Although doctors may not be able to do much medically to help, parents will need their backing to get the child into a special school. They will need advice and perhaps a course of drugs for the child if he becomes very disturbed. Moreover they will need, now and again, the reassurance of having someone to talk to and to have the comfort of knowing that there is someone they can contact in an emergency.

Even if some doctors refuse to recognise the existence of autism it does not alter the fact that the children are there, needing help.

CHAPTER SEVENTEEN

Inheritance

Why should it be that so many autistic children come from middle class families? At one time it was thought that this was because middle class parents were better placed to find specialists who were able to diagnose autism. But the Middlesex survey followed up every child born in Middlesex who was aged 8, 9 or 10 on 1st. January 1964[34] and a number of children who were undiagnosed were found to be autistic. Of these more than would be expected by chance had middle class parents. Alternatively, it was thought that the parents of autistic children were cold and intellectual and that the children withdrew because their parents were not generating the love and warmth necessary for their normal development. There is evidence that less handicapped children are slightly more likely to come from middle class families than autistic children who are more severely handicapped, but only slightly so. The mothers may be articulate and intelligent and it has been remarked that the fathers are frequently people who have got on well in their careers, showing an ability perhaps to canalise their energies to an unusual degree. Many are university lecturers, mathematicians, lawyers or accountants. They may be outstanding amateur astronomers or horologists. It is possible that if their child is mildly handicapped he will have inherited the ability to canalise a single ability to an unusual extent and that his handicap could be an exaggeration of a normal attribute. However, this does not explain the less handicapped child who shows no marked skills nor why the majority of autistic children who are mentally retarded are also more likely to come from these families. Autistic children are, of course, found in all walks of life. Their association with middle class families is interesting from a research point of view, but should not be exaggerated. But it is possible that this now firmly held belief may not be true after all. Lotter's study, because it followed every child, diagnosed or not, born within a circumscribed area, was thought to be unbiased. Others working in this field have also agreed with Lotter.[8, 47] However, recent research is casting doubt on these findings. It will be interesting to discover what further research reveals.[55]

It is not unknown for a family to have more than one autistic child, though this is uncommon. However, the 2% rate of autism in brothers and sisters is 50 times greater than one would expect in the general population. So although it is rare to find a family history of autism, hereditary influences have to be taken into account.[24]

A recent twin study in which at least one twin was autistic has shown that in identical twins it is not unusual for both to be affected. From eleven pairs of identical twins four pairs were both autistic and in these four cases there was no history of brain damage, indicating that autism can be genetically determined. But it was also found that in most identical pairs the co-twin showed some form of cognitive disorder. This would seem to indicate that what is inherited is a form of cognitive abnormality which includes, but is not restricted to, autism and that brain injury can be enough to tip the scale towards autism. Of the ten pairs of fraternal twins, no co-twin was autistic and very few of the co-twins showed any abnormality.[24]

Parents of autistic children often report that a brother or sister is dyslexic or has a similar neurological problem. There has been no systematic investigation but dyslexia is not an uncommon difficulty. Occasionally a cousin is aphasic or has some form of language or speech problem and some families realise, as their own child grows up, that that eccentric uncle or cousin may well be mildly autistic. A young autistic child will not behave in the same way as an older person, unless that person is severely handicapped. Parents of young autistic children will not, at first, be able to relate the behaviour of the autistic adult with that of their young child especially if the adult has made considerable progress. Over time, however, when their child grows and changes and parents begin to understand the underlying handicap better they will be able to recognise the similarities and will realise that the rather odd relative is autistic, even though very mildly. If he is now over 40 it is unlikely that he will have been diagnosed and will probably have managed to scrape by in a small private school perhaps being thought odd, but nevertheless, able to cope.

Take a family which, on one side, has a member who is mildly autistic and is just capable of supporting himself and which on the same side has another who has never taken an interest in fiction or in other pursuits requiring empathy but who is mathematically, scientifically and artistically able and is, moreover, an innovative craftsman. While on the other side is a member who had a reading problem and who had a speech impediment for a while, which may have been caused by making a naturally left handed child use the right hand (a common practice at one time). Does this account for the next generation having problems with dyslexia and autism? Are there two different handicaps within the family or is there a link between them? The twin study shows that cognitive disorders can, in some circumstances, be linked with autism.[24]

Many leads have been investigated, among them being suspected vitamin deficiencies, abnormalities in biochemical functioning, bone formation, blood platelets and heart beat rate but so far nothing very definite has been found. Children may have become autistic after meningitis or encephalitis if they have had these illnesses before the age of 36 months. After four years old, though the child may become handicapped the handicap will not be autism. Some autistic children are known to have sustained brain injuries and a number develop epileptic fits in their teens[24] which would indicate some form of cerebral damage.[24] It is possible that the children who have known 'brain damage' rather than supposed brain dysfunction are more likely to be severely handicapped, though even this has not been firmly established. It may be that autistic children with normal non-verbal intelligence have a different handicap from the severely affected but the evidence is far from decisive at the present time.[50, 51]

It may well be the symptoms spring from several different causes [42] which affect the same part of the brain. This makes no practical difference as far as teachers and parents are concerned as they will need the same kind of care and education. In spite of the interest in this handicap in recent years, little is known for certain except that there is no connection between autism and schizophrenia (or schizophrenia as it is diagnosed in this country) as was once thought.[31] There are as yet no records of autistic children becoming schizophrenic in later life and no records of schizophrenic people having been autistic in childhood. Nor is there more schizophrenia in families with autistic children than would be expected within the normal population. Perhaps fewer as social class and family histories follow a very different pattern.

In most families autism comes as a bolt from the blue, unexpected, unwanted and at first, unrecognised.

CHAPTER EIGHTEEN

Getting Help

How does a parent of an autistic child who is beginning to have doubts about her baby's development get a diagnosis? These days she may have seen an article or TV programme on the subject and may suspect the truth, but it is more likely that she won't recognise the handicap even so. She will see either her GP or the local community doctor, probably both and, as autism is a rare condition, it is possible that neither will realise what the problem is. In the early months, it is doubtful whether they will think that she *has* a problem as the baby will look normal, is likely to have motor milestones within the usual limits, and the mother will have difficulty in defining why she feels uneasy.[58] By the time the child is two, however, it will be becoming obvious that he is handicapped and indeed seriously so. The child may well be 2½ or even 3 before he is referred to a specialist who recognises the handicap and 3½ before the parents being to get their bearings and consider the child's education.

But what then? Specialists may diagnose and suggest that the child attend a nursery group but they will have no idea whether there is one near the parents' home which will be willing to accept a very strange and probably disruptive child; they may suggest education at a special school but will not know if there is one to be found or whether there is an obligation on the authorities to provide a place at one. The parents will not know either and it is unlikely that they will be aware that handicapped children are entitled to education from the age of two (although a suitable school place is not always available). However, as the child is not usually diagnosed until he is 2½–3 years of age and the parents may not begin to look for a school until he is 3½, then the gap in which the child is unprovided for may not be as large as it would at first seem. Although compulsory school age is five most children begin at four. All the same, because of the difficulties of placement many autistic children remain at home far longer than they should. Very few autistic children begin school at two except in one or two areas where the hospitals/clinics/education department and school work very closely together and it has proved possible. It is the fortunate few who get into a special school at a very young age; many do not get a place until they have first been to other unsuitable schools.

How much difference this makes to the final outcome is debatable. Autistic children show a remarkable propensity for catching up with their latent ability at whatever age they start, which accounts for their very rapid improvement when they first go to the right school and their later levelling off. However, they can become very disturbed in behaviour if the school is the wrong one for them and this may take a little while to work through even when they are at last suitably placed. If their handicap is not understood they may also develop secondary symptoms which could have been prevented if they had been able to start at a special school early rather than remaining at home or being wrongly placed. It is obviously an advantage if the children get the correct kind of teaching and understanding from the beginning. Moreover, if they are able to attend school from 2 this will be a terrific help to mothers. They desperately need it at this very difficult time as this is usually the stage when they are so very bewildered and lonely. Anything which can lessen the strain for them during these early years is worthwhile.

Although few children get to a special school at an early age many attend play-groups, nursery classes or kinder-gartens and although these may not be ideal they give the mothers a short break even if this is only for a couple of hours each day.

How do parents find out about diagnosis, special schools, entitlements (such as invalidity benefits) on their own? It is not easy. One local authority department seems to know very little of another department's work, even though they may be under the same roof. Parents usually have to ask, they are seldom told, what the facilities are and how they should apply for them and are apt to find out what is available in a very piecemeal way. Local authorities and specialists are usually not at all good at giving the parents the information they need. Local authorities are sometimes unaware that they have special provision for autistic children within their own boundaries.

It was partly for this reason that the National Society for Autistic Children was formed. It is a clearing house for this kind of information. The Society is becoming better known now and some doctors will suggest to new parents that they get in touch, though is by no means universal.

Parents who suspect that their child is autistic but who cannot get their local GP to refer them to a specialist often contact the Society. They can, of course, change their GP and the Society will advise them of this. Sometimes the GP does not know to whom to refer the child. The Society is not able to disclose the names of specialists to parents as this might be construed as advertising, but they may be able to help. The growing number of hospitals and clinics where autism has been diagnosed and where autistic children have been treated, are known. Once the child is diagnosed the Society is able to give information on special schools and all the other information the parents will need to have. Books and literature on all aspects of the handicap are also available. But above all, parents will want someone they can talk to, especially in the early years or when the child is going through a difficult phase. They may find a social worker who is both kind and knowledgeable and willing to explore avenues that they are unwilling or unable to explore for themselves, but unless the social worker is particularly interested—and most these days carry an enormous and very varied case load—she is not likely to know much about autism or about special schools for autistic children, then there is still a need for someone with whom the mother or father can get in touch who has not only the time to listen but who also knows something of the facilities available, or who is at least able to put the parent in touch with someone who does know. It is an advantage if the person has had some first hand knowledge of autistic children and of the facilities available by having visited at least some of the places for herself. But whoever takes on this work will have to be able to put themselves in the parents' place and do their best to carry out the parents' wishes. Every parent, family situation and child differs, so that if parents feel that they can no longer have the child at home, even during the holidays, then that is their decision and no moral stances or judgements should be made. They should be helped to find permanent residential placement for their child. A severely autistic child can be an almost unbearable burden for brothers and sisters to have to live with. Their possessions may have to be kept locked away to save them from destruction. They may not wish to invite their friends home. They may be teased at school for having a 'mad' brother. The life of every member of the family will have to be considered, not just that of the handicapped child. It may well be that having an autistic child will be too much for some families to endure.

CHAPTER NINETEEN

Joining a Society

Research has shown that only 10% of those with reason to join an association do so. The membership, therefore, of any Society is only the tip of the iceberg. And of those parents who join, not all join for the same reason. Certainly those who joined in the early years became members because they felt that their children could be helped and they wanted to fight to see that special facilities were provided. Now the Society has grown and the facilities with it, the motives in some cases have changed. This is inevitable. As more is provided for the children, parents may look on the Society as an extension of the social services and join to be helped rather than to help.

Professionals may join too. They make up nearly half the membership of the NSAC and most work with the children. A number are students. They join when they are planning an 'in depth' study of autism or writing their thesis for their diploma or degree and, when they leave college or university, unless they work with the children, they are likely to let their membership lapse.

The autistic child who is born to parents who have large well integrated families living near by is fortunate. Their support will be invaluable. Many grandparents, aunts or uncles join the Society. However, these days families are often small and frequently scattered. One pair of grandparents may be unwilling to acknowledge that there is anything wrong with their grandchild, the other pair may be ashamed of him. The parents will find that they are on their own and the Society may be a refuge for them.

Belonging to a Society where parents can meet other parents is probably the best remedy for loneliness. Meeting a parent with similar problems is a joy after trying to explain the child's oddities to friends who have never experienced them. Bringing up an autistic child is a lonely job even if there are understanding grandparents and old friends living near by. Grandparents, though they may love the child, will find his behaviour puzzling; friends may make hurtful comments, usually without meaning to. Parents of handicapped children are a vulnerable target until they learn to grow a thicker skin. Mental handicap and mental illness are poorly understood by the general public—very poorly when one considers that a large number of this same general public will have to spend time in a mental hospital for some form of psychiatric complaint. If one child in a family is mentally handicapped, the other children may come under scrutiny by neighbours who will see significance in even minor events. They may confuse autism with schizophrenia or think that autistic children will grow into psychopaths.

Many parents have been helped by joining the local Society for Mentally Handicapped Children. They may not find another parent of an autistic child, but their son or daughter will be treated with kindness even if the parents and volunteers have no more understanding of his problems than the general public. The main advantage will be that when and if the child learns to enjoy being with others, then there will be outings and parties he can join. Because local Societies for autistic children, except in large towns and cities are of necessity small, not much in the way of entertainment can be arranged on a regular basis. Even small Societies for the mentally handicapped are large in comparison and can provide quite a social life for the child.

Parents are as fond of their handicapped child as they are of their normal children and are even prouder of their achievements. Yet they can seldom talk of them. Their friends with normal children will not understand their pride in what may seem to them a trivial step forward, and they can hardly talk about their achievements to a parent whose child is more severely handicapped.

Parents may be hurt, if they are out with their child, by the way friends and neighbours will try to avoid meeting them, perhaps by crossing the road—and the way that they will ignore the child. Parents would appreciate a glance in his direction. However, they do realise that this behaviour is due to embarrassment and the fact that people just do not know how to behave towards them. This appears to be something that happens to all handicapped people—a blind person may be annoyed when his companion is asked if he takes sugar in his tea. Autistic children lack empathy but normal people are not always very good at putting themselves in another person's place.

However, there is nothing like a few good friends, whether these are parents of autistic children or not. Most friends are loyal and willing to listen. Parents need to talk about their worries. They know that doctors are too busy to listen for long and that relatives may feel too closely involved. They are often constrained by the official visits of the social worker and may feel, unjustly perhaps, that they are being watched for unusual attitudes towards their child, poor household organisation or character faults. They know they may also be expected to relieve their feelings of guilt by talking about them; an attitude rather akin to the famous question 'Have you stopped beating your wife?' Not all parents have these feelings.

But what is meant by guilt? Is it that parents have been made to feel that they have disgraced themselves and their community by having a handicapped child? But some social workers—and doctors—in the early years anyway, did nothing to allay these emotions, they inadvertently exacerbated them. Most parents are lonely, sometimes very unhappy and if they cannot find an appropriate school, desperate. Extra work may exhaust them, misunderstandings by friends and neighbours depress them, but are they suffering from feelings of guilt? Have they said so—or is it just assumed? Has an army of social workers been employed to help assuage feelings that parents do not have or which, in some cases, have been imposed on them? It is far more likely that the parents feel inadequate.

But why do only 10% of parents join? It seems that the

other 90% are non-joiners by nature. And of those who do, not all join for the same reason. Of this 10% many are floating members who join for one year and then lapse. Others lapse and rejoin many times. Some belong for a few years, usually while their child is young, lapsing perhaps losing interest when he goes into long term care. If the child is accepted by a Rudolf Steiner School, for instance, parents will help that organisation and many find that belonging to one association is quite enough for them. Some parents are a long way from help and by keeping in touch feel less isolated. Others become members though they have no wish to become involved. Though some join expecting to get something from the Society, others are excellent fund raisers and have made a lot of money for the Society which has helped to buy the buildings which have become our schools and many parents have willingly given up a great deal of their time helping in various ways.

Yet the only advantage members get over non-members is the quarterly journal and newsletter and, if they belong to a local Society, occasional outings. The Advisory and Information Service is available to all who need it and school places are given to children who are impartially selected and whose local authorities will pay the fees. Belonging to the Society does not guarantee a place at a Society school. Parents may work, however, to start a school in their area so that there is more likelihood that their child will get a place, but they will have to face the possibility that he will not be chosen and that many of the children who are selected will be the children of parents who have done nothing to help, may not be members and may not even be aware that their child is autistic. This seems unbearably unfair to some parents. It *is* unfair but how can the situation be changed? The only way that parents can ensure a place for their child is to have a school where they pay the fees themselves. Very few parents could afford this, however.

The Society is, and has to be, a Society for those who wish to join to help and yet who do not expect to benefit directly themselves. It is also for those who are unable or unwilling to do very much and for those who need the support of others. Associations such as the local Society for Autistic Children can nearly always find work for voluntary helpers, whether they are parents or just those who are interested in the problem and it is a wonderful way of meeting new people and making new friends. A suburban housewife, for instance, may find herself leading quite a different life. If an active role is taken, then it is possible that she will meet a wide variety of people—people she would not have met if she had not been the parent of an autistic child. She will mix with people from a very wide spectrum of the population. It will provide her with new insights and will help her to feel comfortable with everyone from whatever walk in life.

CHAPTER TWENTY

Founding a School

If, within a circumscribed area, there are enough parents without a school for their autistic children who have neither been able to persuade the local authority to provide one, nor to find a place in an independent school, then there is no reason why they should not get together to start one of their own. This may be more easily accomplished with the help of the local Society for Autistic Children—and if there is no local Society, there is no reason why the parents should not start one, with the help of the NSAC. The NSAC has gained much experience in founding schools and will give advice. If the project is a good one, it may even provide a grant or a loan.

The parents will have to establish that there are enough diagnosed children living locally to make the school a viable proposition—and to be classified as a school there must be five children; under five and it will be known as a home teaching unit. However, there is no reason why parents should not begin with a Home Teaching Unit. This way there will be fewer restrictions on the type of building and the number of washbasins and lavatories. It can, in fact, be run from a parent's home. If it is to be a day school, the support of the local authority is essential especially if the school is so situated that only one authority will be able to send children to it. It may be possible, even with a day school, to place it where several authorities have children within daily travelling distance. The viability of the school will be entirely dependent on the willingness of local authorities to pay fees and once a local authority accepts this responsibility, it will also provide transport unless the school is only a short walk from the parents' home.

Local authorities are under an obligation to provide 'suitable' education for all handicapped children and if they have not been able to provide their own school then they must pay for facilities elsewhere. (But in hard times there may be arguments as to what is 'suitable').

If there is the likelihood of financial support, preferably from more than one authority and enough children who are known to be autistic, non-communicating or who would benefit from the same kind of teaching living within a few miles radius, then a few parents—three should be sufficient—should be asked to look for premises in the area. If the school is to be non-residential and is unlikely ever to take more than 6–10 children, then two rooms, cloakroom (including washbasins and lavatories) and kitchen may be sufficient. On the other hand the parents may prefer to buy a house with a view to future growth. The group will have to make sure that they are not infringing any bye-laws, so it would be wise to contact the local health and education departments. The HMI will need to be contacted and will want to see that the rooms are large enough for the proposed number of children and that there is the required number of washbasins and lavatories. The local fire people will also have to visit to satisfy themselves that the school has readily accessible exits and to give advice, with the Building Control Officer, on fire precaution equipment (such as fire escapes, special doors, ceilings or windows) and fire fighting equipment. In the case of a small school, this should not amount to very much. A home teaching unit will probably escape these strictures altogether as, if there are less than five children, it will be considered to be on a parallel with an ordinary household.

Once premises have been found and thought suitable by the parents, then planning permission will have to be sought from the local authority. This usually entails 'change of use'.

There may be objections from local residents to contend with, though this has not been found a problem on the whole. Local planning councils meet usually once a month and sometimes because of pressure of work, matters not dealt with are held over until the next meeting, so it is wise to make an application as soon as a decision has been reached.

When property is changing hands quickly it is necessary to move fast once the matter has been decided. Private buyers can make an instant decision so that suitable properties are often lost. It is imperative, however, to have planning permission, an inspection and a fire report before taking steps to buy unless there is willingness to take a chance on being able to sell again without loss should the building prove unacceptable. It may be that if the school is likely to remain small, the renting of a church hall or the leasing of suitable rooms may be a better proposition.

There are no fixed fees for independent schools. In theory, schools may charge what they like, but in fact, they will have to charge what local authorities are willing and able to pay. There must be realistic costing, allowance being made for inflation and 'contingencies'. Allowance, too, must be made for the fact that the school, however many children it will eventually take, will have to start with five or so only, accepting the remainder gradually, perhaps over a two year period. The overheads will be only slightly less for five children than for twenty, so for the first two years (depending on its size) the school will not break even and this lean time, especially during the first year, will have to be expected. It will be obvious that parents will have to do a lot of fund raising and will find it necessary to apply to Trusts and Foundations for financial backing. Once the school has its full complement of children and if it has been properly costed, its income should match its expenditure. However, the initial cost of buying and equipping the building and the loss it will make in its first year or so will not be recovered. It is useful to find what other schools charge. Schools for autistic children are apt to be more expensive to run than most because of their high staffing ratio.

It is usual to have one teacher and helper to six autistic children and if a maximum of eight children were taken another helper or volunteer might be needed. A lot will depend on how severely the children are handicapped and on the experience and strength of character of the teacher. Even at a small day school it is usual to provide a midday meal and this, too, will have to be taken into account. It may be possible to make some arrangement with a local school. Teaching equipment will be needed, as well as tables and chairs. Some of these items may be donated by manufacturers or local shops and much of the material will have to be adapted by the teacher herself as special teaching equipment for autistic children is not available. (Not infrequently the teacher will have to devise a special learning aid for just one child, who may have a specific difficulty).

In a small school the variability in ages and degree of handicap would seem a big problem but apart from differences in physical size (which will also mean differently sized desks and chairs) this may not present as much difficulty as would be expected. It may not be possible to manage teenage children if they are not only large, but also very disturbed. However, this is not always the case and many can be taught successfully with younger children. Because of the high staff radio and because the children will be receiving quite a bit of individual attention and will be working in small groups, their needs can be recognised and catered for. A small day school should not pose any great administrative problems so long as the children and the fees are forthcoming. The relationship between the parents and the teacher and the teacher and the helper will be all important.

A little more work and determination will be needed when starting a more ambitious project, such as a day and weekly residential school. It will almost certainly be best to buy (instead of rent or lease) a property and large solidly built Victorian houses have been found, by experience, to be especially suitable for this purpose. A house with two inside staircases needs no outside fire escape, for instance, unless the building is very large. A residential project will need much more stringent fire precautions and these can be very expensive indeed. The project committee (which will need to be set up to find a property and when it has found one will guide its adaptation into a school) will need to consider the merits of buying a run down property cheaply but one which will need repair and redecoration, to one that is more expensive, but which, with the necessary alterations expected by the Building Control Office and fire people is almost ready to walk into. It should be borne in mind, too, that after a couple of years, another house in the same road may fall vacant and that it may, by this time, be possible to buy this as an extension. It may be necessary to take out a mortgage but once a school is successfully established, this should not be difficult to arrange. It is probably more convenient if one building is used as the boarding department and the other one as the school.

However, there should be flexibility. A large house built between the wars may serve well. A purpose built school of the semi-fabricated kind is quickly erected and can be tailor-made to suit the children. But the disadvantage with a prefabricated building is that, unlike a house, there may be difficulty in disposing of it if for any reason it has to close. Whatever the building, though, schools run by charitable organisations are only charged half the normal rates and the remaining half is discretionary, so that it is possible that in some areas no rates are charged.

Once planning permission has been obtained, the property has been bought, alterations asked for by the Inspector, fire people and Building Control Officer have been made, the central heating and basic equipment installed—the project committee can be disbanded. At this point two or three people must be asked to serve as Trustees. They will be legally responsible for the financial viability of the school. At this point, too, a Management Committee or Board of Governors will be selected. This committee will meet at least once a term and will usually consist of eight to twelve members who will be chosen for their personal qualities as well as for the section of interest which they represent. There will usually be two or three members who are also members of the organisation that owns the school, and there should be within the membership a parent who has a child at the school. Local interests will probably be represented by a member of the local council in whose area the school is situated, perhaps a local authority educational psychologist. The other members may be a retired head-master, a doctor, solicitor, accountant or architect who live locally. All these people bring their own knowledge and expertise to the running and maintenance of the school.

One of the most important jobs that the management committee will be called upon to do will be to choose, partly from within its ranks also from outside, a group of people who will select the future Principal and perhaps Deputy (depending on the size of the school). The selection of the right person is all important and will affect the whole project for better or for worse. It may not be possible to find someone who has had experience of autistic children though there are more now than there once were. Perhaps the most important point to establish is that the teacher does not think that autism is some form of maladjustment. If this is thought, then the whole approach may be wrong, although if the teacher is perceptive then he or she will see the difference and will change teaching methods accordingly. However, it is best if he or she is a good straightforward teacher who has had experience with handicapped children but who has also taught normal children. Unless the circumstances are exceptional the standard teaching qualifications will be required and normal Burnham Scale rates are paid. In the rush to get a school open (and it is expensive to have it lying empty once it has been purchased) it must be remembered that teachers have to give a term's notice if they are a Principal and half a term's notice otherwise. But it may be wiser in the long run to lose money at this stage rather than to select in haste and repent at leisure. The choice of assistant teachers, helpers and domestic staff will be best be left to the new Principal who will have to work and to be in daily contact with them.

It is informative for the selection panel to find why the applicant wishes to teach autistic children, what he or she thinks autism is and which books have been read. It would show at least some interest if the applicant has sent for some of the NSAC's literature or has taken the trouble to visit a school for autistic children. But if the applicant knows nothing yet is firm, open minded and warm hearted, then he or she may well be the right person. It must not be forgotten either, that in an independent school the headteacher must not only understand the children but will also be responsible for the day to day administration of the school and it may not be easy to find one person who combines these very different qualities. Once appointed, the Principal elect will need to visit schools and units for autistic children to find out as much as possible before taking over. There will also be much to do in the way of selecting staff and ordering stores and equipment, so the backing of the local Society or governing body is essential.

It is most important that the parents and the charitable organisations are known to have nothing whatever to do with the selection of children. When the school is due to open, a psychiatrist or a psychologist with knowledge of autism is appointed to the school and he and the Principal will choose the children. It is unfortunate that the parents who have done the most to help may find that their child is not selected but it is usual to take fees only from local authorities willing to sponsor a child and children who will fit best in age, achievement and behavioural characteristics with the other children.

A weekly boarding school can take children from a much wider area and is not dependent on the goodwill of one or two local authorities. This is all to the good. The school belongs to the Charity and through the Charity to the parents and should reflect their ideas and beliefs. It must be free to make its own policy without interference from the local 'establishment' who may try to enforce their views. If it does good work and is supplying a need then it will get all the co-operation it wants.

A weekly boarding school usually takes children from Monday mornings to Friday afternoons, thereby requiring only half the house staff of a fully residential school. It will also be able to cut down on laundry facilities as parents will be responsible for seeing to the children's heavier items of clothing. The children, too, will see their parents frequently and the parents will not lose their skill in handling the child. It is alarming how quickly a family can close up once a child is away from home for a month or so. To be a workable proposition a day and weekly boarding school must have at least twelve children, preferably more, though no school of this sort should really take more than 25–30 children. There is always the danger of becoming just one more institution.

A fully residential school is a major proposition and should not be attempted by a very small organisation unless it is the only way of finding enough children. It costs a great deal to run and can be more subject to staff problems. Its major advantage is that it is able to take children from all over the country so that parents living in areas where the diagnostic services are poor or who live in sparsely populated rural areas will have the chance of getting their child into the right environment. There will also be families who are only able to cope with a disruptive child for short periods and need a fully residential school for this reason. But the easiest way to begin anything is to start small and build on to it over the years. The first step is always the hardest.

Summary

Why has there been such a very great interest in autistic children, an interest out of all proportion to the number with this handicap? It is probably because there is as yet no known cause and the children, at least when young, look normal and bright with no physical deformities. They are so often handsome children, perhaps because of their look of innocence. This may be because at seven or eight years old, they may possibly have a social age of eighteen months or less, and will therefore not have developed the natural suspicion and 'knowingness' that a normal child, however good natured, will have fostered for his own protection. Although these children are very severely handicapped there is always the feeling, especially among those who have never worked with them, that there must be some quick and easy solution to their problems. This interest is useful if it helps solve the problem of what can be done. The danger is, that when people find that most are severely handicapped and will remain so, they may lose the wish to help.

Autistic children and adults are a minority group and as a minority there will be few facilities especially for them. They remain difficult, sometimes impossible, to integrate into other larger groups for whom adequate provision has been made. It was partly for this reason the Society was formed. But the Society will never have the resources to provide for every autistic child throughout his life. It is therefore necessary, if the parents are to have any peace of mind, that their particular problems should be understood.

All autistic children and adults, from the most severely handicapped, to those few able to lead independent lives, have a very severe communication problem, so severe that they never have an instinctive awareness of the feelings, thoughts and sometimes existence of others. They may learn intellectually that other people have feelings but this does not compensate for their lack of instinct. They may learn how to speak, in much the same way as normal people learn to comprehend and speak a foreign language. They may learn intellectually how to behave socially, but not every behavioural situation can be taught so that their social interaction will be primitive. They may like to be with people but will not be of them. They remain on the outside, not because they wish to be there, but because they do not know how to join in.

This aloneness *is* the handicap and it affects both the less handicapped and those who are severely affected. It is this which indentifies them as autistic. Wherever they are placed—in schools, training centres, hospitals, mixed communities—they remain a group apart. They are at risk from misunderstandings. They may become disturbed over some trifle but will not be aware that it can be corrected with the help of another person, or indeed that they could enlist the help of another person, so that even those who have found a happy environment risk losing it. If they become very disturbed they may be removed from the place where they have been content and put into isolation in the belief that they are suffering from some form of mental deterioration. This will further exacerbate the disturbance and may lead to the over-use of drugs. It is this lack of understanding which worries the parents.

Parents of autistic children are not a breed apart. They behave as they do because they have reason to fear. They realise that their child will not be readily understood and, that when they are no longer able to care for him, he may be placed inappropriately. They fear the indiscriminate use of drugs, the misreading of behaviour leading to unnecessary restraint, and the incorrect estimation of abilities and disabilities which may lead to boredom or stress.

However, most autistic children learn to conform well enough to fit in, though remaining odd. It is the helpless, unhappy vulnerable ones whatever their degree of handicap who should be of concern to all.

Appendix

1. Lorna Wing's 'Handicaps of Autistic Children' will help those not familiar with the condition to recognise it. A detailed list of the characteristic impairments shown by autistic children is given though no child will show *all* of them. The criteria considered by Leo Kanner to be essential for a diagnosis of autism are starred. The more handicapped the child, the more points he is likely to show.
2. The Assessment Scheme devised by Lorna Wing can be useful for both parent and teacher. It will help pinpoint the child's abilities and disabilities and in this way will assist parents and teacher to have some idea of the child's potential and so work out a programme to help him.
3. Elizabeth Newson lists the criteria that must be present for a child to be considered autistic. The points are a modification of Mike Rutter's three points.

Appendix 1

The Handicaps of Autistic Children

A. Basic Impairments

1. *Language Problems*

   (a) Spoken language
   * *(i) Problems in comprehension of speech.
   * *(ii) Abnormalities in the use of speech:
        *Complete absence of speech or, in those children who do speak:
        *Immediate echolalia (a parrot-like repetition of words the child has just heard spoken).
        *Delayed echolalia (repetition of words or phrases heard in the past, often in the accent of the original speaker).

---

*Items essential for a diagnosis of autism as described by Kanner (1943).

*Repetitive, stereotyped, inflexible use of words and phrases.

*Confusion over the use of pronouns.

Immaturity of grammatical structure of spontaneous (not echoed) speech.

Aphasia in spontaneous (not echoed) speech (i.e. muddling of the sequence of letters and words; confusion of words of similar sound or related meaning; problems with prepositions, conjunctions and other small linking words, etc.)

*(iii) Poor control of pitch, volume and intonation of voice.

(iv) Problems of pronunciation.

(b) Non-spoken language and non-verbal communication

*(i) Poor comprehension of the information conveyed by gesture, miming, facial expression, bodily posture, vocal intonation, etc.

*(ii) Lack of use of gesture, miming, facial expression, vocal intonation and bodily posture, etc., to convey information (the only "gesture" may be grabbing someone else's hand and pulling them towards a desired object).

2. *Abnormal Responses to Sensory Experiences*

(i) Abnormal response to sounds (indifference, distress, fascination).

(ii) Abnormal response to visual stimuli (indifference, distress, fascination).

(iii) Abnormal response to pain and cold (indifference, over reaction).

(iv) Abnormal response to being touched (pushing away when touched lightly but enjoying boisterous tickling and romping).

(v) "Paradoxical" responses to sensations (e.g. covering eyes in response to a sound, or ears in response to a visual stimulus).

3. *Abnormalities of Visual Inspection*

(i) The use of peripheral rather than central visual fields (responding to movement and outline rather than to details; looking past rather than at people and things).

(ii) Looking at people and things with brief rapid glances rather than a steady gaze.

---

*Items essential for a diagnosis of autism as described by Kanner (1943).

4. *Problems of Motor Imitation*

(i) Difficulty in copying skilled movements (the child learns best if his limbs are moved through the necessary motions).
(ii) A tendency to muddle left/right, back/front, up/down.

5. *Problems of Motor Control*

(i) Jumping, flapping limbs, rocking and grimacing when excited.
(ii) A springy tip-toe walk without appropriate swinging of the arms.
(iii) An odd posture when standing, with head bowed, arms flexed at the elbow and hands drooping at the wrists.
(iv) Spontaneous large movements, or fine skilled movements, or both may be clumsy in some children, though others appear to be graceful and nimble.

6. *Various Abnormalities of Autonomic Function and Physical Development, Including:*

(i) Erratic patterns of sleeping and resistance to the effects of sedatives and hypnotics.
(ii) Erratic patterns of eating and drinking, including consumption of large quantities of fluid.
(iii) Lack of dizziness after spinning round.
(iv) Immaturity of general appearance and unusual symmetry of face.

B. Special Skills (contrasting with lack of skill in other areas)

*1. Skills that do not involve language, e.g. music, arithmetic, dismantling and assembling mechanical or electrical objects, fitting together jig saws or constructional toys.

*2. An unusual form of memory which seems to allow the prolonged storage of items in the exact form in which they were first perceived, (e.g. phrases or whole conversations spoken by other people), poems, long lists (e.g. of all the kings of England) long passages of music, the route to a certain place, the arrangement of a collection of pebbles, the steps to be followed in a routine activity, a complicated visual pattern, etc. The items selected for storage do not appear, on any criteria used by normal people, to be of any special importance, and they are stored without being interpreted or changed.

*Items essential for a diagnosis of autism as described by Kanner (1943).

C. Secondary Behaviour Problems

*1. Apparent aloofness and indifference to other people, especially other children, although enjoying some forms of active physical contact. Some autistic children, even under 5 years of age, show attachment, on a simple physical level, to adults they know well but are indifferent to children of their own age. N.B. This problem may diminish or disappear with increasing age though relationships with understanding adults are always much better than those with peers.

*2. Intense resistance to change and attachment to objects and routines. A fascination with regular repeated patterns of objects, sounds, routines, etc. The collection, for no apparent purpose, of objects such as plastic bottles, pebbles, knobs from biros. Older children who have a good vocabulary and some command of grammatical constructions may be fascinated by certain topics, e.g. electricity, astronomy, birds; they ask repeated questions and demand standard answers. The interest is not a creative one, but is repetitive and stereotyped in form.

3. Inappropriate emotional reactions. These include lack of fear of real danger, but excessive fear of some harmless objects or situations; laughing, weeping or screaming for no apparent reason; laughing when someone else is hurt or another child is scolded. These reactions result from lack of comprehension of the meaning of the situations.

*4. Poverty of imagination:

(a) Inability to play imaginatively with objects, toys or other children or adults; or to imitate other people's action in an imaginative, creative way. Lack of understanding of the purpose of any pursuits which do not bring an immediate and obvious sensory reward and of those which involve an understanding of words and their complex associations, e.g. school work, games, hobbies, social conversation, literature, poetry, etc. There is a consequent lack of motivation to indulge in these activities, even if the necessary skills are available to the child.

(b) A tendency to select for attention minor or trivial aspects of things in the environment instead of an imaginative understanding of the meaning of the whole scene, e.g. attending to one ear ring instead of a whole person, a wheel instead of the whole toy train, a switch instead of the whole piece of electrical apparatus, reacting to the needle used for an injection while ignoring the person who is giving it.

---

*Items essential for a diagnosis of autism as described by Kanner (1943).

(c) Absorption in repetitive activities such as stereotyped movements, touching, tasting, smelling and manipulating objects and, sometimes, self injury.

5. Socially immature and difficult behaviour, including running away, screaming in public, biting or kicking other people, grabbing things off counters in shops, making naïve and embarrassing remarks.

It is unusual to find children who have all the problems mentioned in the list. Many combinations of items in addition to the classic Kanner's syndrome will be found if a large number of children suspected of being autistic are observed. It is of intellectual interest to decide which children fit Kanner's description and which do not, but, in practice, the prescription of education depends upon the specific impairments, special skills and behaviour problems shown by the child and not upon the label that is given to him. If impairments affecting both comprehension and use of spoken and non-spoken language are present, then the type of education suitable for autistic children will be necessary, whether or not the child is classically autistic.

Appendix 2

Notes on Using the Assessment Scheme

When recording a child's behaviour it is important to describe what he actually does and not to give either theoretical interpretations or guesses about "hidden potential". The child's responses should be observed by setting up the appropriate situation. Thus his comprehension of speech and of gesture can be tested in the classroom by giving him instructions of varying complexity when an appropriate occasion arises. Concrete examples should be given; for example, it is more informative to note that a child climbs to the top of all the wall bars in the gymnasium with remarkable speed than simply to say that he climbs with agility. The assessment cannot be completed until the teacher has had the child in her class long enough to see how he behaves in the relevant situations. The actual length of time necessary varies with different children.

If it is not possible to say whether a certain type of behaviour is present, this should be recorded as "don't know". Sometimes "not applicable" has to be used, for example for the abnormalities of speech in children who are mute.

For each abnormality of behaviour, the frequency of its occurrence and its severity should be noted.

If required, standard forms for recording observations could be designed to suit the requirements of any individual school or unit and included in the child's case notes. If this is done, space should be left for illustrative descriptions of behaviour.

When children are living at home and attend school daily, some information, such as the pattern of sleeping, will have to be obtained from the parents. Parents can in fact use the scheme to describe the behaviour of their child at home. The contrast between home and school is always of interest and may give clues to improving methods of teaching and management in both situations.

A Standardized Scheme for Assessment

I. Language (spoken and non-spoken)

Spoken

(a) Comprehension of speech

    (i) Does the child respond to his own name? Does he point to some familiar objects when asked? Does he obey very simple instructions in a familiar context (e.g. "give me your cup"). Do you ever send him out of the room to fetch one familiar object? Could he be sent out for two or three things? Does he obey a sequence of commands "first do this, then this, then this"? Does he obey instructions needing decisions, ("if ___, if not ___")? Can he understand past and future tenses as well as present?

    (ii) Does he have any problems with prepositions? e.g. Does he look in the right place if told "it is under the cupboard" as well as "it is *in* the cupboard"?

    (iii) Does he comprehend better if instructions are sung to a tune instead of spoken?

(b) Use of speech

    (i) If the child does not talk, does he make any noises? Does he babble like a baby? Do his noises have a conversational intonation? Do any of his noises have a definite meaning?

    (ii) If he says some words, are these just parrot-like echoing? Does he name any objects or people when asked? Does he name some things spontaneously? Does he join two words together? Does he make longer phrases but miss out the small linking words? Does he make complete sentences? Does he use past, present and future tenses?

(c) Pronunciation

    (i) How clearly does the child speak? Can he be understood by people who know him well, or by strangers?

(d) Intonation

    (i) Does the child use intonation to aid expression—e.g. in asking questions, in showing puzzlement, hesitation, etc., or is his intonation always the same?
   (ii) Does he control the loudness and pitch of his voice?
  (iii) Does he ever use a special voice, different from his usual one?

(e) Echolalia

    (i) Does the child immediately repeat words or phrases spoken by other people in a parrot-like meaningless way?
   (ii) Does the child repeat words or phrases used by other people some time after he has heard them? Does he talk to himself using these repeated phrases?

(f) Stereotyped use of phrases

    (i) Does the child confuse pronouns, e.g. saying "you" when he means "I"?
   (ii) Does the child use words and phrases in a rigid, stereotyped way, e.g. referring to something by using the word or phrase first associated with it, such as "you—paint—it" for scaffolding or "you can't have that red pot" whenever any request made by the child is refused?

(g) "Aphasia"

    (i) Does the child muddle the sequence of letters in words (e.g. diccifult = difficult)?
   (ii) Does the child muddle the sequence of words in sentences (e.g. Take park to dog. Put salt it on)?
  (iii) Does the child confuse words that are opposites or are usually paired (e.g. on and off, yes and no, sock and shoe, mummy and daddy)?
  (iv) Does the child hesitate and search for words when talking spontaneously?

Non-spoken

(h) Comprehension of non-spoken communication

    (i) Does the child respond to concrete clues in the situation—e.g. does he know he is going out when he sees his coat? Does he understand pointing and beckoning? Does he respond to a simple mime such as a finger on the lips to mean "quiet"? Does he respond to complex mime such as pretending to eat, drink, brush hair, etc?

  (ii) Can his behaviour be controlled by his teacher's facial expressions without using speech, e.g. by smiles or frowns? Do these have to be exaggerated for him to respond?

  (iii) Does he respond to a nod or a shake of the head to mean yes or no, unaccompanied by speech?

(i) Using non-spoken communication

  (i) If the child cannot speak, how does he get things he wants? Does he just scream; get everything for himself; pull other people by the hand; point by touching; point from a distance; use mime and gesture to indicate his needs; or a mixture of these methods?

  (ii) Does the child have a range of facial expressions? Does he just look happy or miserable, or can he look surprised, puzzled, enquiring, etc?

  (iii) Does he nod or shake his head, clearly meaning yes or no? Does he use other gestures such as "thumbs up" to indicate success or approval?

Spoken or non-spoken

(j) Social communication (by speech, gesture, miming or sign language)

  (i) Does the child point things out to other people and want them to look? Does he spontaneously talk about things that have happened to him? How often does he do this and how much detail does he give? Does he tend to repeat the same things or does he tell of new things as they happen?

  (ii) Does the child answer questions (by speech or by nodding and shaking of the head)? Does he do it reluctantly or willingly? Does he ever engage in a conversation? Are his contributions stereotyped and repetitious, or can he converse freely and change the subject appropriately? Does he converse about things outside his own immediate experience?

  (iii) Does he ask questions? Are these limited to his own needs or does he ask questions because of curiosity? Does he ask questions about things outside his own personal experience? Are his questions repetitive and stereotyped, or do his questions show a creative developing interest?

  (iv) Does he talk to, or otherwise communicate with children of his own age? Does he do this reluctantly or willingly?

II. Responses to sensory stimuli

(a) Sounds

(i) Does the child ignore some sounds? Do some distress him? Do some fascinate him?

(b) Visual stimuli

(i) How does he react to lights and shiny objects?
(ii) Does he twist and flick his hands or objects near his eyes?
(iii) Does he like to watch things spin?
(iv) Does he seem to concentrate on one aspect of an object or person and ignore the rest, e.g. electrical switches, circular shapes, people's teeth?
(v) Does he seem to identify things and people by their outline rather than by the details of appearance?

(c) Pain, heat and cold

(i) Does the child ignore pain, heat or cold? Is he oversensitive?
(ii) Does he deliberately injure himself in any way?

(d) Sensations of bodily movement

(i) Does he especially enjoy rapid movement, e.g. swings, slides, round-abouts, etc?
(ii) Does he spin himself round? Does he become giddy when he does this?
(iii) Does he rock, jump or show other stereotyped movements?

(e) Touch, taste and smell

(i) Does he tend to explore objects and people through touch, taste and smell?

(N.B. If there is a possibility that the child may be deaf or partially sighted, the teacher's observations can provide useful evidence. It should be noted if the child responds consistently to some sounds or some visual stimuli. The nature of these stimuli and the circumstances in which the child responds should be described.)

III. Movement, gait and posture

(i) How does the child walk? Does he swing his arms? Does he walk on tip toe? Does he look odd and awkward? Is he particularly graceful in spontaneous movement?
(ii) Is he dexterous or clumsy in his fine finger movements?
(iii) Is his posture odd or awkward in any way?

   (iv) Can he copy other people's movements? Does he wave good-bye? Does he clap? Are these movements easy or are they stiff and awkward? How easily does he learn gymnastic exercises, dances, miming games, etc? Does he confuse up/down, back/front, right/left when trying to copy?

   (v) How does he behave when excited? Does the excitement produce movements of his whole body, including face, arms and legs?

IV. Social responses

   (i) How many people could the child recognize and respond to if he met them in an unfamiliar context? No one? His parents only? His teachers? A circle of friends and neighbours?

  (ii) How does the child respond to gentle touches, to cuddling, to rough-and-tumble games?

 (iii) How does the child respond to social approaches without physical contact?

  (iv) Does he show affection to others spontaneously?

   (v) How does he respond to children of his own age as opposed to adults? Does he have any friends of his own age?

  (vi) How does the child make eye contact? Does he have a blank, unfocused stare? Does he avoid making eye contact at all? Does he give brief flashing glances only? Does he stare too long at times? Is his eye contact better with people he knows than with strangers?

V. Emotional responses

   (i) Does he have any special fears?

  (ii) Does he seem unaware and unafraid of some real dangers?

 (iii) Does he sometimes laugh or seem very distressed for no reason at all?

  (iv) Does he show any response to other people's feelings, e.g. would he be sympathetic if someone had an accident? Would he be aware if someone felt miserable or ill?

VI. Resistance to change and attachment to objects and routines

   (i) How does the child respond to changes in the daily routine? Does he insist upon exact repetition of some or all of the daily programme, e.g. the same route for the daily walk, everyone at the same place at table, etc?

  (ii) Does he carry out rituals of his own, e.g. tapping on a chair before sitting down, touching everything on the table before eating, etc?

(iii) Does he arrange objects in special ways, e.g. in long lines or patterns? Does he replace things in the exact position from which they came, down to the smallest detail?

(iv) Is he attached to particular objects which must accompany him everywhere? How does he react if the object is lost? Does he collect any type of object in what seems to be a completely purposeless way, e.g. holly leaves, detergent packets, segments of rubber beach balls, etc?

(v) Does he have an obsessive, repetitive, uncreative, stereotyped interest in certain subjects, e.g. the planets, electricity, bodily functions, etc?

(vi) Is his play repetitive and stereotyped, e.g. does he continually manipulate the same objects in the same way; play the same record again and again; re-do the same puzzle repeatedly; perform the same series of physical actions, perhaps for hours at a time?

VII. Play and amusements

(i) How well can the child handle objects and constructional toys? Does he roll things along the floor? How many bricks can he build into a tower? Can he use screw toys? Can he do in-set puzzles or real jig saw puzzles? How many pieces? Does he make things with constructional toys? Can he follow the printed diagrams with, for example, Lego or Bilofix?

(ii) Does he have any imitative or imaginative play? Does he use real objects for their correct purpose? Does he copy his mother in domestic tasks? Does he give people pretend cups of tea in toy tea sets? Does he play with cars or trains as if they are real, e.g. putting cars into a garage, shunting the trains, etc? Does he play with toy animals or dolls as if they are real? Does he kiss them, put them to bed, hold dolls' tea parties, play school with them, etc? Does he pretend to be, e.g. a cowboy, policeman, nurse, etc., acting out an imaginary game, not just wearing the costume?

(iii) Does he play imaginatively with other children, e.g. doctors and nurses, mothers and fathers, cowboys and Indians, etc? Does he take an active part or is he always passive and not contributing to the fantasy?

(iv) Does he join in co-operative play that does not need fantasy, e.g. chasing; circle games like ring a roses; hide-and-seek; ball games played without rules; games with rules like football; table games.

(v) What types of outings does he enjoy?

(vi) What does he watch on television?

(vii) Is he interested in stories read aloud?

(viii) Does he enjoy listening to music? Can he sing in tune? Can he play any instrument?

VIII. Difficult or socially immature behaviour

(i) Does he run away or wander?

(ii) Is he destructive?

(iii) Does he scream frequently or for long periods, or have temper tantrums?

(iv) Is he aggressive to adults or to children?

(v) How does he behave in public? Does he grab things in shops; scream in the street; make naïve remarks; feel people's clothing, hair or skin, etc?

(vi) Does he tend to be less active than other children, or is he overactive?

(viii) Does he resist whatever you try to do for him or automatically say no to any suggestion?

IX. Special skills found in classically autistic children

(a) Non-language dependent skills

(i) Does the child have any special skills in dismantling, assembling or manipulating mechanical or electrical objects?

(ii) Does he have any outstanding musical skill? Does he have absolute pitch?

(iii) Can he do lengthy calculations in his head?

(b) Outstanding memory

N.B. The classic autistic child remembers things exactly as they were first experienced, with little or no appreciation of their real significance.

(i) Does the child remember verbal material, e.g. poems, songs, lists of names, details of a subject which especially interests him, unusually well?

(ii) Does he notice if any object, however small or unimportant, is moved from its usual position?

(iii) Does he seem to recognize routes and places with unusual accuracy? Does he remember details of maps, etc. with unusual accuracy?

(iv) Does he remember numerical material unusually well, e.g. multiplication tables, the dates of events, days on which dates fall, train timetables, etc?

X. Self care

(a) Mobility

(i) Can the child walk without help? Can he run as well as other children of his age?

   (ii) Can he walk upstairs and downstairs without help?

  (iii) Is he able to climb with agility?

  (iv) Can he pedal a tricycle or a bicycle?

(b) Feeding

   (i) Does he have to be fed, or can he feed himself with his fingers, a spoon, spoon and fork, or knife and fork? Can he help himself to food when at table? Can he cut a slice of bread from a loaf?

  (ii) How good are his table manners?

 (iii) Are there any problems with chewing?

  (iv) Does he dribble?

   (v) Are there any marked food fads?

  (vi) Does he suck or swallow inedible objects?

(c) Washing

   (i) Can he wash and dry his own hands, or his hands and face? Can he bath himself with or without help?

  (ii) Is he aware when his hands or face are dirty?

(d) Dressing

   (i) Can the child put on any of his garments by himself? Can he do up buttons and laces?

  (ii) Can he remove any of his garments? Can he undo buttons or laces?

 (iii) Can he brush and comb his own hair?

  (iv) Can he brush his own teeth?

   (v) Is he concerned if his clothes are dirty or untidy?

(e) Continence

   (i) What stage has he reached in his toilet training in the daytime?

  (ii) Is he clean and dry at night?

(f) Independence

   (i) Can the child get objects that he wants for himself? Does he look for things that are hidden? Does he climb on a chair to reach things? Does he undo door handles and locks?

  (ii) Is he aware of any dangers, e.g. from hot things, sharp things? Is he aware of the danger of heights or of deep water? Is he aware that traffic is dangerous? Does he know how to cross a road safely?

 (iii) How much does he have to be supervised? Could he be allowed to go into another room alone; in the garden alone; in the street outside the house; around the local neighbourhood; or farther afield? Could he travel on public transport alone?

XI. Sleep

(i) Does the child usually stay awake till very late at night or wake up very early in the morning? (Note usual times of going to sleep and waking.)

(ii) Is his sleep usually disturbed? Does he scream, or demand attention in other ways when he wakes in the night?

XII. Achievements in school work

(a) General aspects

(i) Length of attention span for different types of task.

(ii) Motivation for different types of tasks.

(b) Specific skills

N.B. In each case the child's ability to understand as well as to execute the tasks should be assessed.

(i) Pre-reading skills, including ability to recognize objects in pictures.

(ii) Reading.

(iii) Writing.

(iv) Number work; money; measurement.

(v) Telling the time; days of the week; months of the year; giving the date.

(vi) Drawing; painting; modelling.

(vii) Is the child able to cope with any school subjects beyond the basic skills, e.g. geography, biology, etc.?

XIII. Domestic and practical skills

(i) Does the child help with laying and clearing the table; tidying up; cleaning; washing up; washing clothes, etc.? Can he use domestic equipment such as a vacuum cleaner? Does he help with shopping?

(ii) Can he help with any aspect of preparing and cooking food?

(iii) Can he knit or sew?

(iv) Can he do woodwork?

(v) Can he do any other craft work?

XIV. Other problems

Any abnormalities not covered in the other sections.

XV. The child's own personality

However handicapped a child is, he has his own personality which affects the way he reacts to his impairments of function. Autistic children are no exception. Despite all their problems it is possible to see that, for example, some are basically tough and outgoing, others are shy and timid, some are confident while others are anxious. Careful consideration of this aspect is important because it should guide the way in which the techniques of teaching are applied.

Practical applications of the observations

Describing a child's behaviour by using the above scheme does not provide any overall assessment such as a developmental level or an intelligence quotient. All it can do is to give a standardized approach to defining a child's specific impairments, social handicaps, behaviour problems and any compensating skills as an essential part of a general medical and psychological assessment. It can, however, be of considerable assistance in the differential diagnosis. Children with the behaviour pattern characteristic of Kanner's autistic syndrome, as given in Chapter 1, can be identified. If a child has severe problems in comprehending and using speech but has the ability to communicate his needs by gesture and mime then the possibility of deafness or a specific developmental receptive speech delay should be investigated with special care. If a child does not talk but appears to have good comprehension of speech, can use non-spoken communication and has some imaginative play, then a developmental expressive speech delay should be suspected. Sometimes a child reveals practical and even academic skills in the familiar situation of home or classroom even though he has performed badly on standard intelligence tests. This finding indicates the need for further psychological investigations with particular attention to motivating the child to perform as well as he can.

When the assessment is completed it will be possible to see which problems stand out as most urgent. The results of the first observations should not be taken as the final indication of the child's abilities but should be used as the starting point for a programme of teaching skills and management of behavioural abnormalities. The full assessment, or else the parts relevant to the individual child, can be repeated at intervals in order to evaluate progress and the success or failure of the teaching techniques that are being used.

Appendix 3

Elizabeth Newson gives the three points which must be present for a child to be considered autistic. They are:

(1) Impairment of language.
(2) A failure of social empathy.
(3) Rigidity and inflexibility of thought processes.

References

As this is not intended to be a text book, the list of references is not exhaustive. However, most of the books and papers listed below have extensive bibliographies which will enable those who wish to find out more to follow up the aspects in which they have a special interest.

1. ALTER, J. DEWEY, M. and EVERARD, P. (1975). The autistic adult in the community. *Proceedings of NSAC 7th Annual Meeting and Conference*. San Diego.
2. ASPERGER, M. (1944). Die autistischen psychopathen im Kindersalter. *Arch für Psychiatric und Nervenkrankenheiten. 117* 76.
3. BARTAK, L., RUTTER M. and COX, A. (1975). A comparative study of infantile autism and specific developmental receptive language disorder. 1. The Children. *British J. Psychiatry. 126* 127.
4. BARTAK, L. and RUTTER, M. (1976). Differences between mentally retarded and normally intelligent autistic children. *J. Autism and Childhood Schizophrenia. 6* 109.
5. BOUCHER, J. (1976). Is autism primarily a language disorder? *British J. of Disorders of Communication. 11* 135.
6. BROWN, R. (1965). *Social Psychiatry* Macmillan London.
7. BURGESS, J. (1978). The school leaver and adult. *Communication. 12* 33.
8. CANTWELL, D. P., BAKER L. and RUTTER, M. (1978). Family factors *in* M. RUTTER, E. SCHOPLER (eds) *Autism: A Reappraisal of Concepts and Treatment*. Plenum Press, New York.
9. CARR, J. (1976). The severely retarded autistic child *in* L. WING (ed) *Early Childhood Autism*, second edition. Pergamon Press, Oxford.
10. CHURCHILL, D. W. (1971). Effect of success and failure in psychotic children. *Arch of General Psychiatry. 25* 208.
11. COX, A., RUTTER, M., NEWMAN, S. and BARTAK, L. (1977). A comparative study of infantile autism and specific developmental receptive language disorder 2. Parental characteristics. *British J. of Preventive and Social Medicine. 31* 131.
12. CRYSTAL, D. (1970). Prosodic systems and language acquisition, *in* P. LEON (ed) *Prosodic Feature Analysis*. Didier, Paris.
13. DEMYER, M. K., BARTON S., ALPERN, G. D., KIMBERLIN, C., ALLEN, J., YANG, E. and STEELE, R. (1974). The measured

intelligence of autistic children. *J. Autism and Childhood Schizophrenia.* *4* 42.

14. DEWEY, M. (1974). Address to the Annual General Meeting of the NSAC (U.S.A.). Reprinted in *Communcation.* *8* 56.
15. DEWEY, M. and EVERARD, P. (1974). The near-normal autistic adolescent. *J. Autism and Childhood Schizophrenia.* *4* 348.
16. DEWEY, M. (1976). Courtship Communication. A paper prepared for the Allen M. Meyers Foundation and reprinted in *Communication.* *12* 48.
17. DEWEY, M. (1976). The autistic person and religion. A paper prepared for the Allen M. Meyers Foundation and reprinted in *Communication.* *12* 56.
18. ELGAR, S. (1976). Organisation of a school for autistic children. *in* M. P. Everard (ed). *An Approach to Teaching Autistic Children.* Pergamon Press, Oxford.
19. ENGLEFIED, R. (1976/77). *Language, its Origin and Relation to Thought.* G. A. Wells and D. L. Oppenheimer (eds) Elek/Pemberton, London.
20. EVERARD, P. (1975). A hypothesis. *Communication.* *9* 34.
21. EVERARD, P. (1976). The chicken or the egg. *Communication.* *10* 58.
22. EVERARD, P. (1976). The mildly handicapped autistic person. A paper read at the International Symposium at St. Gallen, Switzerland.
23. EVERARD, P. (1977). Non-communication. *Communication.* *11* 13.
24. FOLSTEIN, S. and RUTTER, M. (1977). Infantile autism. A genetic study of 21 twin pairs. *J. Child Psychol. Psychiat. 18* 297.
25. GOULD, J. (1976). Assessment: The role of the psychologist *in* M. P. Everard (ed). *An Approach to Teaching Autistic Children.* Pergamon Press, Oxford.
26. GRIFFITHS, C. P. S. (1969). A follow-up study of children with disorders of speech. *British J. Disorders of Communication.* *4* 46.
27. HEMSLEY, R. and HOWLIN, P. (1976). The management of behaviour problems. *in* M. P. Everard (ed). *An Approach to Teaching Autistic Children.* Pergamon Press, Oxford.
28. HERMELIN, B. and O'CONNOR, N. (1970). Psychological Experiments with Autistic Children. Pergamon Press, Oxford.
29. KANNER, L. (1943). Autistic disturbances of affective contact. *Nerv. Child. 2* 217.
30. KANNER, L. (1946). Irrelevant & metaphorical language in early infantile autism. Am. J. Psychiatry. *103* 242.
31. KOLVIN, I. (1971). Psychosis in childhood—a comparative study *in* M. Rutter (ed) *Infantile Autism: Concepts, Characteristics and Treatment.* Churchill Livingstone London.
32. LENNEBERG, E. M. (1967). *Biological Foundations of Language.* Wiley, New York.

33. LOCKYER, L. and RUTTER, M. (1969). A five to fifteen year follow-up study of infantile psychosis 3. Psychological aspects. British J. of Psychiatry. *115* 865.
34. LOTTER, V. (1966). Epidemiology of autistic conditions in young children and prevalence. *Social Psychiatry. 1* 124.
35. McGLONE, J. (1976). Sex differences in the cerebral organisation of verbal functions in patients with unilateral brain lesions. *Research Bulletin 399.* Universtiy of W. Ontario.
36. McNEILL, D. (1966). Developmental psycholinguistics *in* F. Smith and G. A. Miller (eds). *The Genesis of Language.* M.I.T. Cambridge Mass.
37. MITTLER, P. GILLIES, S. and JONES, E. (1966). Prognosis in psychotic children. Report of follow-up study. *J. Ment. Def. Res. 10* 73.
38. NEWSON, E. (1977). Diagnosis and early problems of autistic children. *Communication. 9* 43.
39. RICKS, D. M. (1972). *The Beginning of Verbal Communication in Normal and Autistic Children,* (M.D. Thesis), London.
40. RICKS, D. M. and WING, L. (1976). Language communication and the use of symbols *in* L. Wing (ed). *Early Childhood Autism,* second edition. Pergamon Press, Oxford.
41. RIMLAND, B. (1965). *Infantile Autism,* Methuen, London.
42. RUTTER, M. (1966). Behavioural and cognitive characteristics of a series of psychotic children. *in* J. Wing (ed). *Early Childhood Autism.* Pergamon Press, Oxford.
43. RUTTER, M. and LOCKYER, L. (1967). A five to fifteen year follow up of infantile psychosis. Description of sample *British J. Psychiatry. 113* 1169.
44. RUTTER, M., GREENFIELD, D. and LOCKYER, L. (1967). A five to fifteen year follow-up study of infantile psychosis 2. Social and behavioural outcome. *British J. Psychiatry. 113* 1183.
45. RUTTER, M. and BARTAK, L. (1973). Special educational treatment of autistic children. A comparative study 2. follow-up findings and implications for services. *J. Child Psychol. Psychiat. 14* 241.
46. RUTTER, M. (1974). The development of infantile autism. *Psychol. Med. 4* 147.
47. RUTTER, M. (1975). A comparative study of infantile autism and specific developmental receptive language disorder 2. Parental characteristics. *British J. Psychiatry. 126* 146.
48. RUTTER, M. TIZARD, J. YULE, W., GRAHAM, P. and WHITMORE, K. (1976). Research Report, Isle of Wight studies 1964–74. *Psychological Medicine. 6* 313.
49. RUTTER, M., YULE, W. BERGER, M. and HERSOV, L. (1977). An evaluation of a behavioural approach to the treatment of autistic

children. Final Report to the Department of Health and Social Security, London.

50. RUTTER, M. (1978). Language disorder and infantile autism *in* M. Rutter and E. Schopler (eds). *Autism: A Reappraisal of Concepts and Treatment.* Plenum Press, New York.

51. RUTTER, M. (1979). Language, cognition and autism, R. Katzman (ed). *Congenital and Acquired Disorders.* Ravel Press, New York.

52. RUTTER, M. (1979) Autism: Psychopathological mechanisms and therapeutic approaches *in* M. Borther (ed). *Cognitive Growth and Development Essays in Memory of Herbert G. Birch.* Bronner/Mazel Inc., New York.

53. SCHOPLER, E. (1971). Parents of psychotic children as scapegoats. *J. Contemp Psychother. 4* 17.

54. SCHOPLER, E. (1976). Towards reducing behaviour problems in autistic children. *in* L. Wing (ed). *Early Childhood Autism* second edition. Pergamon Press, Oxford.

55. SCHOPLER, E., ANDREWS, C. E. and STRUPP, K. (1979). Do autistic children come from upper middle class parents? *J. of Autism and Developmental Disorders. 9* 129.

56. TREVARTHEN, C. (1974). Conversations with a two month old. *New Scientist. 62* 230.

57. TUBBS, V. K. (1966). Types of linguistic disability in psychotic children. *J. Ment. Defic. Res. 10* 230.

58. WING, L. (1976). Diagnostic, clinical description and prognosis *in* L. Wing (ed). *Early Childhood Autism.* Second edition. Pergamon Press, Oxford.

59. WING, L. (1976). Epidemiology and theory of aetiology *in* L. Wing (ed). *Early Childhood Autism.* Second edition. Pergamon Press, Oxford.

60. WING, L. (1976). Remedial education for autistic children *in* L. Wing (ed). *Early Childhood Autism.* Second edition. Pergamon Press, Oxford.

61. WING, L. (1978). Overview. *Communication. 14* 24.

62. WOLF, S. and CHESS, S. (1964). A behavioural study of schizophrenic children. *Acta Psychiat. Scand. 40* 438.

Index